REVIVAL OR JUDGMENT?

How Idolatry is Destroying the Church in
America and God's Call to Repentance

Pray for revival!

Randall Corey

BY RANDALL L. COREY

Revival or Judgement?
How Idolatry is Destroying the Church in America and God's Call to
Repentance
by Randall L. Corey

Printed in the United States of America.

ISBN 9781498495486

Unless otherwise indicated, Scripture quotations taken from the New
International Version (NIV). Copyright © 1973, 1978, 1984, 2011 by
Biblica, Inc.™. Used by permission. All rights reserved.

www.xulonpress.com

"If My people, who are called by My name, will humble themselves and pray, and seek My face and turn from their wicked ways, then I will hear from heaven, and will forgive their sin and will heal their land" (2 Chr. 7:14 NIV).

PREFACE

D r. A.W. Tozer said that if the Holy Spirit were completely taken from the church today, it would continue on as if nothing happened and "nobody would know the difference." That is the present situation in many of America's churches. The purpose of this book is to call God's people to repentance and prayer for revival. My title refers to "The Church." If we believe in Jesus Christ as our Lord and Savior, then we are members of one body, His bride, the Church. It does not matter from which denomination you come. Denominational differences and denominational traditions have divided the body of Christ long enough. It is time for believers to focus on the evil one and how he is destroying our country, not on condemning each other. It should be apparent to anyone who knows Jesus Christ as Lord and Savior that America is at a turning point. We are calling good evil and evil good in our country. We have banned prayer in schools, legalized abortion, legalized same-sex marriage, erected a portal to Baal in New York City, and now have pending lawsuits for people who want to marry animals. Legalizing polygamy will soon be a congressional or Supreme Court matter, and if there is no moral standard, every sexual deviancy condemned in scripture will be legalized by our legislators and our court system.

Republicans or Democrats are not responsible for this moral crisis. Followers of Jesus Christ are responsible for the moral climate of our nation, and we, the Church, have failed. Regardless of denominational or doctrinal differences we must unite as we repent of our nation's sins and ask God for a fresh outpouring upon the Church of Jesus Christ. One of the meanings of the word "intercession" is to stand in someone else's shoes. We must own the sins of America as if we had committed them because we are responsible for the moral breakdown in our country! We are responsible for seeking God for a new outpouring of his Spirit! *"If My people, who are called by My name, will humble themselves and pray, and seek My face and turn from their wicked ways, then I will hear from heaven, and will forgive their sin and will heal their land"* (2 Chr. 7:14). We must act on our responsibility, repent, and seek God for a fresh outpouring.

You might question what right I have to write this book. I am writing this book because I have repented and turned from the sins that are destroying our nation. I came out of a suicidal spirit, alcoholism, and homosexuality in 1989. Since 1993 I have been running support groups for those coming out of various types of sexual addiction. When it comes to the brokenness in the American family, I have not only experienced it, but I've heard numerous stories of broken family patterns that have taken men and women into sin. And I am referring to church families. My ministry targets Christians who are struggling with addictions.

I have also experienced the denominational condemnation that exists between various churches. This book is written from a charismatic viewpoint, but I was reared as an independent, fundamental, Baptist who was taught that God didn't do miracles anymore, in spite of the fact that God healed my great-grandfather from terminal cancer as his Baptist pastor and deacons laid hands on him and prayed. Please do not take offense at any references I make to healings or miracles as I quote Scripture. This merely continues the problem of doctrinal division. We do not need that division to continue! Feel free to disagree with some of my statements, but do not disagree that God's people need to pray and seek revival in spite of your individual doctrinal beliefs. Denominational and racial division in the church of Jesus Christ needs to stop! We must unite around our Savior, and love one another as He loves us! May God have mercy on America and on our denominations as we repent of our sin and seek His face.

TABLE OF CONTENTS

CHAPTER 1

GOD'S COVENANT WITH ABRAHAM AND AMERICA

This United States of America is an absolutely unique country. Other than the nation of Israel, there has never been another nation dedicated to serve the true God of heaven in freedom from its foundation. When people make a covenant with God, God keeps His word and fulfills His promises. When people break their promises to the God of heaven, God judges the nation. I think it is absolutely essential that we understand that what is happening in America now already happened to Israel. Portions of this book will upset people from different denominational backgrounds, but that is not my purpose. My purpose is to call the American Church to repentance that leads to revival. I do not pretend to be all knowing. There is content in this book that can be challenged, and that is not totally accurate according to other surveys or statistics. But if you keep in mind the overall purpose of this book is repentance for our nation and promoting a new revival for America, many of my subjects will make sense whether or not they are 100% accurate or correct.

Before we can understand why our country is endangered by our present moral climate, it is important that we understand God's covenant to Abraham, called "Abram," until God changed his name. God made a covenant with Abram promising him descendants and the land that we now call Israel. Abram obeyed and journeyed to Israel in obedience to God from his home in Ur of the Chaldees. The fulfillment of this "promised land" came with some conditions that weren't very pleasant. The promise given Abram for the land is as follows: *Genesis 16:13-16: "Then the LORD said to him, 'Know for certain that for four hundred years your descendants will be strangers in a country not their own and that they will be enslaved and mistreated there. But I will punish the nation they serve as slaves, and afterward they will come out with great possessions. You, however, will go to your ancestors in peace and be buried at a good old age. In the fourth generation your descendants will come back here, for the sin of the Amorites has not yet reached its full measure.'"*

God told Abram that his descendants (not yet born) would be out of the land for four hundred years, and would be enslaved in another country. He also promised that they would be freed from this bondage and come back to this "promised land" with great possessions. The Scripture states that this would last for four generations, or the equivalent of 400 years at this point in history. The part of this Scripture from Genesis that I want to bring to our attention is, *"for the sin of the Amorites has not yet reached its full measure."* God, in His mercy, was giving the Amorites (the collective tribes living in the land promised to Abram) four hundred more years to repent before He evicted them from their land and destroyed them. It is also interesting to me that our history, with the founding of the Jamestown settlement in 1607, will reach the 410-year mark in 2017. From this assertion we must understand that God is merciful, patient, and compassionate. But we must also understand that God will judge sinful nations. I believe that God is withholding judgment on our land. We deserve His wrath for what we are doing, and for what we have done, but Father God is merciful. In His mercy, He is calling the church in America, His people, to repent and avoid His judgment.

So what were the sins of the Amorites that caused them to lose their land to the people of Israel? The most specific sin was sexual idolatry. Let's examine what Scripture has to say about this. After the giving of the law, the book of Leviticus, chapter 18, specifically states why the land was being purged of its inhabitants. (I encourage you to read the entire chapter.) After a huge listing of sexual sins, including incest, adultery, homosexuality, bestiality, and human sacrifice of children, Leviticus 18:24-30 states, *"'Do not defile yourselves in any of these ways, because this is how the nations that I am going to drive out before you became defiled. Even the land was defiled; so I punished it for its sin, and the land vomited out its inhabitants. But you must keep my decrees and my laws. The native-born and the foreigners residing among you must not do any of these detestable things, for all these things were done by the people who lived in the land before you, and the land became defiled. And if you defile the land, it will vomit you out as it vomited out the nations that were before you. Everyone who does any of these detestable things—such persons must be cut off from their people. Keep my requirements and do not follow any of the detestable customs that were practiced before you came and do not defile yourselves with them. I am the* LORD *your God.'"* America has put itself under the same curse that these Gentiles suffered. We are committing the same, idolatrous, sexual sins and United States of America is going to vomit out its inhabitants. We are incurring the judgment of God.

Idolatry as Sexual Uncleanness: Baal, Ashtoreth, and Molech

Most of us western people are more familiar with the Greek or Roman Gods through exposure to reading mythological literary collections in school. As we read archeological documents we understand that there eventually emerged many related and localized gods and goddesses throughout the eastern world preceding the Greek and Roman counterparts. These were usually associated with worshipping the sun, moon, stars, or creatures. Paul describes in *Romans 1:21-25: "For although they knew God, they neither glorified him as God nor gave thanks to him, but their thinking became futile and their foolish hearts were darkened. Although they claimed to be wise, they became fools and exchanged the glory of the immortal God for images made to look like a mortal human being and birds and animals and reptiles. Therefore God gave them over in the sinful desires of their hearts to sexual impurity for the degrading of their bodies with one another. They exchanged the truth about*

God for a lie, and worshiped and served created things rather than the Creator—who is forever praised. Amen." So what is the first indicator that we have forsaken the knowledge of God? Sexual immorality is the first indicator. This is a description of how when we refuse to acknowledge God our Creator, we turn to worshipping creation. The first thing that follows this idolatry is sexual immorality and degrading our bodies with our impurity.

We find no Scriptural acknowledgements of idolatry after the flood. After the erection and destruction of the tower of Babel and following the dispersion of the tribes from the tower of Babel, we begin to see false worship rising up. I believe this is why God called Abram from Ur of the Chaldees to Canaan, a land where his father had previously purposed to move. The Canaanite people of the land had slipped into idolatry. Abram's response to God's promise to give him the land was to build an altar and worship the LORD (Gen 12:7). This demonstrates the true worship of the God of Heaven dating back to Abel after the fall of Adam and Eve. This true worship is something God always honors. In John 4, Jesus stated to the woman at the well that, *"...a time is coming and has now come when the true worshipers will worship the Father in the Spirit and in truth, for they are the kind of worshipers the Father seeks. God is spirit, and his worshipers must worship in the Spirit and in truth."* This is the worship that Father God expects from us. Jesus was the ultimate and final sacrifice for our sins, and when we despise His kingdom, the works of our hands will be destroyed.

When we consider the gods and goddesses of the people of Canaan, we find several mentioned by name in Scripture: Baal, Ashtoreth, and Molek (Molech). Other versions or related names of these gods are also found in numerous archeological findings throughout the Middle East and in Africa. It would seem that their origins were common, but historically their worship and supposed attributes varied among different people groups. We will examine the origins and characteristics of these gods as it relates to Israel and the land of Canaan that God promised to give Abraham.

Baal

In Genesis we first see the name "Baal" combined with a ruler's name, *"When Shaul died, Baal-Hanan son of Akbor succeeded him as king." (Gen. 36:38-39).* In Exodus we begin to read locations named after this god: *Baal Zephon* (Ex.14:2) and *Bamoth Baal* (Ex. 22:41). Baal was usually a phallic deity (male penis) associated with fertility, but worship and attributes varied by localities. Baal was also worshipped as the "sun god."

Easton's Bible Dictionary[1] offers the following notes and Scriptures about Baal: *"Baal–lord. (1.) The name appropriated to the principal male god of the Phoenicians. It is found in several places in the plural BAALIM (Judg. 2:11; 10:10; 1 Kings 18:18; Jer. 2:23; Hos. 2:17). Baal is identified with Molech (Jer. 19:5). It was known to the Israelites as Baal-peor (Num. 25:3; Deut. 4:3), was worshipped till the time of Samuel (1 Sam 7:4), and was afterwards the religion of the ten tribes in the time of Ahab (1 Kings 16:31-33; 18:19, 22). It prevailed also for a time in the kingdom of Judah (2 Kings 8:27; comp. 11:18; 16:3; 2 Chr. 28:2), till finally put an end to by the severe discipline of the Captivity (Zeph. 1:4-6). The priests of Baal were in great numbers (1 Kings 18:19), and of various classes (2 Kings 10:19). Their mode of offering sacrifices is described in 1 Kings 18:25-29. The sun-god, under the general title of Baal, or "lord," was the chief object of worship of the Canaanites. Each locality had its special Baal, and the various local Baals were summed up under the name of Baalim, or "lords." Each Baal had a wife, who was a colourless reflection of himself."*

In Numbers 25 we see the first Scriptural mention of Baal worship linked to God's people, Israel, and sexual immorality. Numbers 25: 1-3 *"While Israel was staying in Shittim, the men began to indulge in sexual immorality with Moabite women, who invited them to the sacrifices to their gods. The people ate the sacrificial meal and bowed down before these gods. So Israel yoked themselves to the Baal of Peor. And the LORD's anger burned against them."* We specifically see here that bowing and sacrificing to Baal meant engaging in sexual immorality or orgies (feasting and immorality). God's wrath was immediately unleashed against the Israelites and 24,000 people died in a plague. This "yoking" themselves specifically refers to the sexual immorality that went with the worship of this god. Revelation 2:14 gives some further revelation about this Israeli idolatry, *"Nevertheless, I have a few things against you: There are some among you who hold to the teaching of Balaam, who taught Balak to entice the Israelites to sin so that they ate food sacrificed to idols and committed sexual immorality."* This Scripture specifies that Balaam advised Balak to entice the Jews to enter into the sexual idolatry of Baal worship, involving sexual immorality with pagan women.

Ashtoreth

The first mention of Ashtoreth in Scripture is in Judges 2:12-14, *"They forsook the LORD, the God of their ancestors, who had brought them out of Egypt. They followed and worshiped various gods of the peoples around them. They aroused the LORD's anger because they forsook him and served Baal and the Ashtoreths. In his anger against Israel the LORD gave them into the hands of raiders who plundered them. He sold them into the hands of their enemies all around, whom they were no longer able to resist."* Notice that the worship of Ashtoreth is associated with Baal. As earlier stated in the quote from <u>Easton's Bible Dictionary</u>, *"Each Baal had a wife, who was a colourless reflection of himself."* Ashtoreth was also often a goddess of fertility. With some historical statues, she was depicted as a "many breasted" goddess.

The <u>Jewish Encyclopedia</u>[2] in an article by Morris Jastrow, Jr., and George A. Barton asserts that, *"Astarte is the Phenician name of the primitive Semitic mother-goddess, out of which the most important of the Semitic deities were developed. She was known in Arabia as "Athtar," and in Babylonia as "Ishtar." Her name appears in the Old Testament (I Kings xi. 5; II Kings xxiii. 13) as "Ashtoreth," a distortion of "Ashtart," made after the analogy of "Bosheth" ... Solomon is said to have built a high place to her near Jerusalem, which was removed during Josiah's reform (I Kings xi. 5, 33; II Kings xxiii. 12). Astarte is called in these passages "the abomination of the Zidonians," because, as the inscriptions of Tabnith and Eshmunazer show, she was the chief divinity of that city (see Hoffmann, "Phönizische Inschriften,")...*

18

In Phenician countries she was the female counterpart of <u>Baal</u>, and was no doubt worshiped with him by those Hebrews who at times became his devotees. This is proved by the fact that Baalim and Ashtaroth are used several times (Judges x. 6; I Sam. vii. 4, xii. 10)...

The <u>International Standard Bible Encyclopedia</u>[3] states, *"In Babylonia and Assyria Ishtar was the goddess of love and war...The other goddesses of Babylonia, who were little more than reflections of the god, tended to merge into Ishtar who thus became a type of the female divinity, a personification of the productive principle in nature, and more especially the mother and creatress of mankind. The chief seat of the worship of Ishtar in Babylonia was Erech, where prostitution was practiced in her name, and she was served with immoral rites by bands of men and women."*

Please notice that this prostitution was both male and female. This gives us more understanding of the passage from 1 Kings 14:23-25 which asserts, *"They also set up for themselves high places, sacred stones and Asherah poles on every high hill and under every spreading tree. There were even male shrine prostitutes in the land; the people engaged in all the detestable practices of the nations the LORD had driven out before the Israelites."* This idolatry included homosexual behavior.

Molek (Molech)

The first scriptural reference to Molek occurs in Leviticus 18. The 18th chapter gives a long list of sexually unclean actions, and vs. 21 says, *"Do not give any of your children to be sacrificed to Molek, for you must not profane the name of your God. I am the LORD."* After this long list of sexual prohibitions including homosexuality, lesbianism, bestiality, and murdering children, God specifically says, *"Do not defile yourselves in any of these ways, because this is how the nations that I am going to drive out before you became defiled. Even the land was defiled; so I punished it for its sin, and the land vomited out its inhabitants... Keep my requirements and do not follow any of the detestable customs that were practiced before you came and do not defile yourselves with them. I am the LORD your God."* It is intriguing that God specifically states here, as He did earlier to Abram, you are getting the land because I am taking it away from these peoples because of their sin.

In the <u>Jewish Encyclopedia,</u> in an article by Isidore Singer, and George A. Barton, we read the following information: *"The name "Molech," later corrupted into "Moloch," is an intentional mispointing of "Melek," after the analogy of "bosheth" (comp. Hoffmann in Stade's "Zeitschrift," iii. 124). As to the rites which the worshipers of Molech performed, it has sometimes been inferred, from the phrase "pass through the fire to Molech," that children were made to pass between two lines of fire as a kind of consecration or februation; but it is clear from Isa. lvii. 5 and Jer. xix. 5 that the children were killed and burned. The whole point of the offering consisted, therefore, in the fact that it was a human sacrifice."*

It is completely clear from secular and Biblical history that the worship of Molek involved the sacrifice of children. They were burned to death, often in the arms of this god, who was sometimes built as a furnace with outstretched arms. In Joshua 6:26, Joshua curses and prophecies over Jericho after he destroyed it saying, *"Cursed before the* LORD *is the one who undertakes to rebuild this city, Jericho: At the cost of his firstborn son he will lay its foundations; at the cost of his youngest he will set up its gates."* The fulfillment of this word is given us in I Kings 16:34: *"In Ahab's time, Hiel of Bethel rebuilt Jericho. He laid its foundations at the cost of his firstborn son Abiram, and he set up its gates at the cost of his youngest son Segub, in accordance with the word of the LORD spoken by Joshua son of Nun."* This tells us some more information about the purposes of sacrificing to Molek. These sacrifices were often committed to keep a city safe from attackers. Archaeologists have uncovered ashes and bones of children in city gates of many Middle-Eastern historical sites who were sacrificed to Molek to seemingly assure the safeguarding of a city.

In some later chapters we will discuss how this same idolatry relates to the current state of our nations in America, Canada, and Europe in relation to abortion. Let's conclude with the third reminder of Father God's opinion of these broken sexual practices and this sacrificing of children. In Leviticus 18 God says, *"'And if you defile the land, it will vomit you out as it vomited out the nations that were before you. Everyone who does any of these detestable things—such persons must be cut off from their people. Keep my requirements and do not follow any of the detestable customs that were practiced before you came and do not defile yourselves with them. I am the* LORD *your God.'"*

21

[1] Easton, Matthew George, Easton's Bible Dictionary, [Illustrated Bible Dictionary], (1897), is in the public domain and may be freely used and distributed.

[2] Jewish Encyclopedia (1901-1906) The Jewish Encyclopedia is in the public domain and may be freely used and distributed.

[3] Orr, James, editor, International Standard Bible Encyclopedia, 1939, William B. Erdmans publishing company, 2140 Oak Industrial Dr. NE, Grand Rapids, MI 49505

Chapter 2:

What is Idolatry?

For most Americans the term "idolatry" has no modern application or context. At best we may think of the ancient temples to gods and goddesses where people prayed to statues of the local deities. It's hard for us as a modern, western civilization to realize that idolatry doesn't necessarily have to do with bowing down before a statue, or bringing gifts and making sacrifices to an idol. So what is a good definition of idolatry for modern people?

Let's start with standard dictionary definitions of idolatry. Merriam-Webster's Online Dictionary[1] defines idolatry as: *1. the worship of a physical object as a god 2. immoderate attachment or devotion to something.*] Webster's New World Dictionary: Third College Edition[2], defines idolatry as: *1. worship of idols 2. excessive devotion or reverence for some person or thing.*

The only parts of these dictionary definitions of idolatry that may help us to grasp that idolatry isn't necessarily bowing down to a statue is the definition that idolatry can be *"immoderate attachment...or excessive devotion or reverence for some person or thing."*

Strong's Concordance with Hebrew and Greek Lexicon[3] #8655 (1890) lists the Hebrew word for "idolatry" as "אָרַף"(*tĕraphiym*). *It is translated "idolatry, idols, image(s), teraphim, family idol;" and it refers to, "a kind of idol used in household shrine or worship."* In the New Testament Paul tells believers to *"...flee idolatry" (I Cor. 10:14)*. The Greek word used here is "εἰδωλολατρεία" (eidōlolatreía) which according to Thayer's Greek Lexicon[4] (1890) means, *"Image worship-literally or figuratively; or formal sacrificial feasts; or the vices that spring from idolatry."* This really isn't at all helpful for us except for the "vices" part, which we may understand from the Scriptures we've already viewed referring to sexual vices or uncleanness. It puts us right back at bowing down to something which is not a general practice in our modern culture. But we must ask ourselves, why did they bow down to these statues and what were the "vices" involved? What benefits did they think they were gaining? Why did they leave the worship of the Creator God of the heavens and the earth for a statue they made with their own hands?

To answer this question we must ask ourselves, "Why were we created and what is our purpose as human beings?" Genesis 1:26 says, *"Then God said, "Let us make mankind in our image, in our likeness, so that they may rule over the fish in the sea and the birds in the sky, over the livestock and all the wild animals, and over all the creatures that move along the ground."* The first thing we learn is that we were created in the image of God, and that He created us to "rule," or "have dominion." We also learn from Genesis 3:8 *"Then the man and his wife heard the sound of the LORD God as He was walking in the garden in the cool of the day, and they hid from the LORD God among the trees of the garden. ⁹ But the LORD God called to the man, "Where are you?"* It's obvious from this Scripture that we were made to fellowship with our Creator. I personally believe it was the pre-incarnate Jesus who called to them. God came to be with Adam and Eve. Who we are and what we were made to be originated with our Heavenly Father. Our identity comes from Him. The Westminster confession states our purpose this way: *"Man's chief end is to glorify God, and to enjoy him forever.* 1 Corinthians 10:31(KJV) states, *"Whether therefore ye eat, or drink, or whatsoever ye do, do all to the glory of God."* It seems obvious that Adam and Eve were to be in fellowship with God and take their identity as children from Him. Our identity as human beings should come from the same source-our Heavenly Father. Anything else from which we attempt to define ourselves or give meaning to our lives is idolatry.

I think our best definition of idolatry as westerners might be based on this thought: Idolatry is anything we use to attempt to assert who we are (personal identity) other than knowing God and fellowshipping with Him as we take our sense of being from living in His love. This can only happen through a restored relationship with our Heavenly Father through the redemption that is ours in Yeshua Homashia, Christ Jesus, the Messiah, the Lamb of God. Anytime I attempt to define myself outside of these boundaries I am bowing myself to something from which I am attempting to gain self-value or identity. That is idolatry. I could be seeking many things: power, riches, fame, love, sexual fulfillment; but all of these things outside of a vibrant relationship with God become hollow empty tombs encasing me in death and separation from God's love and relationship. Within the boundaries of a healthy relationship with our heavenly Father, none of the aforementioned things are wrong, specially when we use them to glorify Him. That was His intention in creating us with desires that could be pleasurable and righteously fulfilled.

[1] By permission. From Merriam-Webster's Collegiate® Dictionary, 11th Edition ©2016 by Merriam-Webster, Inc. (www.Merriam-Webster.com).

[2] Webster's New World Dictionary: Third College Edition, By permission. © 1988 by Simon and Schuster Inc.

[3] Strong, James, Strong's Concordance with Hebrew and Greek Lexicon, 1890, is in the public domain and may be freely used and distributed.

[4] Thayer, Joseph Henry, Thayer's Greek Lexicon, 1889, is in the public domain and may be freely used and distributed.

CHAPTER 3

SEXUAL IDOLATRY AND SIN IN AMERICA'S CHURCHES

Although we do not have statues to Baal, Ashtoreth, and Molek in American churches as Israel did in the Temple, it is obvious to anyone with common sense that we are worshiping these sexual idols in the body of Christ. Sexual sin is rampant throughout the church regardless of denominational affiliations or connections. Here are some topics that I feel reflect our idolatrous relationships and some statistics to back up my assertions.

Divorce

I am beginning this chapter with the subject of divorce because I feel it is one of the most important pictures of our relationship with Jesus Christ as His bride. Depending on whose statistics one looks at, one-third or one-half of Christian marriages end in divorce. God hates divorce.

Malachi 2:15-16:*" Has not the one God made you? You belong to him in body and spirit. And what does the one God seek? Godly offspring. So be on your guard, and do not be unfaithful to the wife of your youth. 'The man who hates and divorces his wife,' says the LORD, the God of Israel, 'does violence to the one he should protect,' says the LORD Almighty. 'So be on your guard, and do not be unfaithful.'"*

Divorce was only allowed in Hebrew marriages on the wedding day if the bride was not a virgin. Adultery meant death in the Hebrew culture, which is not a part of our Grace covenant completed through Jesus. In the year 2000, a Barna report stated the divorce rate in the evangelical church is near 35%. Here's a quote from the Barna survey: *"The Barna Research Group's [2000] national study showed that members of nondenominational churches divorce 34 percent of the time in contrast to 25 percent for the general population. Nondenominational churches would include large numbers of Bible churches and other conservative evangelicals. Baptists had the highest rate of the major denominations: 29 percent. Born-again Christians' rate was 27 percent. To make matters even more distressing for believers, atheists/agnostics had the lowest rate of divorce 21 percent."* [1]

On another side note, I think the lower divorce rate among non-church people has to do with the lower marriage rate in our general culture. A very high percentage of people in the general population simply cohabitate. Cohabitation is also becoming more frequent in the church. Marriage occurs more often where people are taught that marriage is the representation of Christ and His church. God has no expectation of unbelievers respecting and keeping the precepts of His word. But Jesus said in John 14:15, *"If you love me, keep my commands."* Our perspective and focus is on the Church of Jesus Christ keeping the precepts of God's Word. God's first and only expectation for unbelievers is that they should repent and receive His gift of salvation through Jesus Christ.

There is another problem with divorce in the church, and it has to do with the church's approval of divorced Christians remarrying. In the New Testament remarriage is only allowed if my spouse is dead. Jesus said in Matthew 19:19, *"I say to you: whoever divorces his wife, except for sexual immorality, and marries another, commits adultery."* In Matthew 5:32 which is the Sermon on the Mount, Jesus also said, *"But I tell you that anyone who divorces his wife, except for sexual immorality,* [discovered on the wedding day in Jewish tradition] *makes her the victim of adultery, and anyone who marries a divorced woman commits adultery."* In First Corinthians 7:39 the apostle Paul informs us that remarriage is allowed only upon the death of spouse: *"A woman is bound to her husband as long as he lives. But if her husband dies, she is free to marry anyone she wishes, but he must belong to the Lord."* This is not a statement of condemnation for anyone who is divorced and remarried. Grace to you! Keep your present covenant. If that is your situation, make the most of your marriage relationship. Worship and honor God together! But the scriptures make it very plain that remarriage is not allowed after a divorce unless our spouse is dead. The Scriptures are very clear. If you divorce you are to remain unmarried unless your spouse dies.

Some pastors use the "except for sexual immorality," quote as grounds for divorce and remarriage. It should be clear from the other scriptures quoted that this is a mistaken belief. Knowledge of the Hebrew tradition behind divorce is necessary to understand the proper interpretation of these Scriptures. Traditionally Jewish marriages are consummated at the wedding ceremony in a tent that is erected for the couple for sexual consummation. We see an application of this principle in the birth of Jesus. Joseph was considering divorcing Mary, because an engagement was as binding as a wedding. Joseph knew she was pregnant, and he knew the child was not his because they had not been sexually intimate. The Angel of the Lord appeared to him and straightened this out for him. At a Jewish wedding, a white garment is placed under the couple. When the hymen in the female is broken in the consummation there is bleeding. After the couple leaves the tent, this garment with the blood on it is shown to prove that the woman was a virgin. If it was found that she was not a virgin, this constituted grounds for divorce on the spot.

The other problem associated with divorce or adultery is the problem of children having one parent in the home. Children with no father in their home are twenty times more likely to go to prison than those living with both parents. *"The proportion of births to unmarried women has increased greatly in recent decades, rising from five percent in 1960 to 32 percent in 1995. After some stability in the mid-1990s, there was a gradual rise from 1997 through 2008, from 32 to 41 percent. The rate appears to have stabilized again, and was at 40 percent in 2014."*[2]
"Fewer than half (46%) of U.S. kids younger than 18 years of age are living in a home with two married heterosexual parents in their first marriage. This is a marked

*change from 1960, when 73% of children fit this descrip-
tion, and 1980, when 61% did, according to a Pew
Research Center analysis of recently released American
Community Survey (ACS) and Decennial Census data."*

We have reared a generation of orphaned children
with living parents.

Pornography in the Church

Not only is divorce a huge issue in the church, pornography is also. The porn industry generates about $13
billion each year in the U.S. and globally about $97 bil-
lion. According to some surveys, the number one cause of
divorce in Christian marriages is now pornography. One
of the most overwhelming sexual problems in the body
of Christ is the problem of pornography in the church.
Here are some statistics from a <u>Focus on the Family</u>
article: *"Christians aren't immune. When surveyed, 53
percent of men who attended Promise Keepers said they
viewed pornography that week.* [This statistic was from
the year 2000-it's worse now!] *More than 45 percent of
Christians admit that pornography is a major problem in
their home. An anonymous survey conducted recently by
<u>Pastors.com</u> reported that 54 percent of pastors admitted
viewing porn within the last year. In an online newsletter,
34 percent of female readers of <u>Today's Christian Woman</u>
admitted to intentionally accessing Internet porn. One out
of every six women who read <u>Today's Christian Woman</u>
say they struggle with addiction to pornography (Today's
Christian Woman, Fall 2003)."* [3] Please notice that these
statistics are 13 years old; the problem is worse now.

As you can see many of these statistics are out of date. The problem is exacerbated in 2016. Here are some general American stats from 2014: *"64% of American men view porn at least monthly; the percentage of Christian men is nearly the same. 79% of men ages 18-30 view porn at least monthly. 67% of men ages 31-49 view porn at least monthly. 55% of married men view porn at least monthly. (Digital journal, August 14, 2014)."*

The problem is not just in American men; the problem is also in church leadership, namely pastors. *"Fifty-one percent of pastors say pornography is a possible temptation. Nearly 20% of the calls received on Focus on the Family's Pastoral Care Line are for help with issues such as pornography and compulsive sexual behavior. And of the 1,351 pastors that Rick Warren's website, Pastors. com, surveyed on porn use, 54% said they had viewed internet pornography within the last year and 30% of those had visited within the last 30 days."* [4] Are there some within the other 46% struggling and not admitting it?

Fornication Before Marriage Among Christians

Some fairly recent statistics seem to demonstrate that the modern generation has very little consideration for the apostle Paul's admonition in I Cor. 6:18 to, *"Flee fornication."* The following information was taken from a poll involving 2600 participants between the ages of 18 to 59. *"According to the '2014 State of Dating in America' report published by Christian Mingle and JDate, 61 percent of Christians said they would have sex before marriage. Fifty-six percent said that it's appropriate to move in with someone after dating for a time between six months and two years.*"[5] The statistics of this poll reflect the outright rebellious and disobedient attitude of single believers in the Church of Jesus Christ.

Some of you may be objecting that the above statistics only represent one survey, so here are statistics from another survey. *"In fact, a recent study reveals that 88 percent of unmarried young adults (ages 18-29) are having sex. The same study, conducted by <u>The National Campaign to Prevent Teen and Unplanned Pregnancy</u>, reveals the number doesn't drop much among Christians. Of those surveyed who self-identify as 'evangelical,' 80 percent say they have had sex.*"[6] I challenge you to go online and look at the statistics yourself. There are numerous surveys done by various agencies that assert the same problem. Single Christian people are prolifically having sex before marriage.

Adultery in Marriage Among Christians

When we turn from single people to look at married people, the statistics about immorality do not improve. In a 2014 survey, Joel Hesch, the founder of Proven Men Ministries, put forward these statistics: *"Furthermore, the born-again group proved not much better than the general consensus of Christians that included nominal believers when it comes to infidelity, as nearly a third of the self-proclaimed born-again Christians admitted to having an extramarital sexual affair while they were married."*

It is hard to find accurate, up-to-date surveys on these statistics. Surveys are usually anonymous, but we also have to wonder about the honesty of those being surveyed. What is shocking for me in these statistics is the high rate of admissions to adultery. If someone was trying to put up a front as a Christian, I would not expect a positive admission to sin because I have worked with men struggling with addictions. From experience I know addicts are extremely well polished liars. Here are some more statistics that also include women and pastors. This was copied from a 2008 article: *"As many as 65 percent of men and 55 percent of women will have an extramarital affair by the time they are 40, according to the Journal of Psychology and Christianity. A Christianity Today survey found that 23 percent of the 300 pastors who responded admitted to sexually inappropriate behavior with someone other than their wives while in the ministry."*[7] Whatever the actual percentage rates are, it is obvious that adultery is a huge problem in the Christian church, and pastors are no exception.

Tolerance of Homosexuality and Lesbianism in the Church

A survey of American congregations done by Duke University and the University of Chicago has statistics to share that show further tolerance for sexual sin. *"The report, 'Changing American Congregations,' is part of the ongoing National Congregations Study (NCS). The Pew Research Center's Religion & Public Life Project contributed funding to the study, which involved inter-views with a clergyperson or other key member of each of the 1331 congregations surveyed. The survey found that between 2006 and 2012, the share of congregations allowing an openly gay or lesbian couple to become full-fledged members grew from 37% to 48%. In addition, the number of congregations that allowed openly gay and lesbian members to assume any lay leadership position also increased – from 18% in 2006 to 26% in 2012."* [8] The statistics from this survey covered a six-year period and were released in 2014.

Another PEW research survey released in 2015, gives more specific statistics for evangelicals. *"Most Mormons and evangelical Protestants still say homosexuality should be discouraged by society – in line with the teachings of many of their churches – but 36% of both groups say it should be accepted. Among Mormons, there was a 12-point increase (from 24% to 36%) in acceptance since 2007, and among evangelicals there was a 10-point rise (from 26% to 36%). Jehovah's Witnesses remain perhaps the most opposed of any U.S religious tradition toward homosexuality, with just 16% saying it should be accepted by society."* [9] In my opinion, the reason the acceptability rate is increasing among evangelicals is because of the increase of homosexual behavior among their own family members due to family breakdowns.

Another shocking trend is the attempt to normalize homosexuality in several major denominations. The United Methodist Church in America took the following steps after their 2016 conference: *" The United Methodist Church (UMC) took a major step toward a possible reorganization on Wednesday, creating a commission to decide whether the largest American mainline Christian denomination should restructure so it can ordain LGBT people and allow pastors to officiate same-sex marriages."* [10] The Southern Baptist Convention also has a struggle with some of its churches attempting to ordain gay ministers, or marry homosexual partners. This is causing a great deal of division in the SBC convention.

Here is a fairly comprehensive list of churches who have ordained gay ministers: *"The Metropolitan Community Church, a predominantly LGBT church, has ordained LGBT candidates for ministry since its founding in 1968. In 1972, the United Church of Christ, became the first mainline Protestant denomination in the United States to ordain an openly gay clergy. Other churches are the evangelical Lutheran Church in America, (since 2010) and the Presbyterian Church USA (since 2012). The Episcopal Church in the United States, and the Christian Church (Disciples of Christ) have also allowed ordination of openly gay and lesbian candidates for ministry for some years."[11]*

This is not a condemnation of anyone struggling with same-sex attraction. It is no different than any other sin. As I already stated in my preface, I came out of homosexuality. Jesus' love and grace is extended to anyone, but God's word is clear that marriage and sex is between a man and a woman. The qualifications for elders are also very clear in Scripture. Gay couples or singles are not qualified for church leadership when living in sin.

The Worship of Molek thru Abortion in the Church

January 22, 2017, will be the 43rd anniversary of legalized abortion in the United States, and since then, well over 58 million preborn babies have been killed by abortion. The totals continue to increase by almost 3,000 a day. But you might protest that these statistics represent our entire society, and you are right. But here are some modern-day statistics that hopefully will shock you. *"The newly released research, [2015] conducted by Christian research group <u>LifeWay</u> at the behest of pro-life group <u>Care Net</u>, paints a very different picture of those seeking abortions than you might imagine. The study interviewed 1,038 women who had received an abortion. Surprisingly, a full 70 percent of these women were Christian."* [12]

These statistics make it very clear that abortion is happening in the body of Christ. Christians are murdering babies. This rate of abortion is also clearly connected to the rates of immorality in the church.

Political Threat from Abortion

There is a political perspective to Western European and the American abortion rates. In 1960, American families averaged 3.7 children per family. This was a decline from the earlier 20th Century as rising middle class people decided to have fewer children to save money. In the year 2014, American families averaged 1.9 children per family. When we come to Western European countries, some of the rates are even lower than America's birth rate. So what is the political perspective here? Radical Islam does not intend to take over Western European nations or the United States through radical jihad only. There is a plan by Muslim countries to integrate Europe and America and to have huge families. This will enable them to take over our societies by democratic vote. The average number of people in a European_Muslim family is 8, with many families having 10 to 14. This does not take into account increased family size by polygamy. By increasing the number of Muslims living in democratic countries, they will become the dominant population force in that country. As their people go into public life, they can be elected to prominent positions and then democratically change the laws of that country to suit the Muslim ideology. This has already occurred in the Detroit suburb of Dearborn, Michigan, where Muslims dominate the city council. Before his death, Libyan Leader Mu'ammar Al-Qaddafi stated this: *"We have 50 million Muslims in Europe. There are signs that Allah will grant Islam victory in Europe–without swords, without guns, without conquests. The fifty million Muslims of Europe will turn it into a Muslim continent within a few decades."* This is already happening in the countries of France and Germany. Abortion has more consequences than God's judgment upon our land and other countries.

Food as an Idol

Any bodily appetite outside of God's boundaries is sin. Proverbs 20:19-21 says, *"Listen, my son, and be wise, and set your heart on the right path: Do not join those who drink too much wine or gorge themselves on meat, for drunkards and gluttons become poor, and drowsiness clothes them in rags."* Obesity is not just an American problem, it is rampant in the church. There are numerous studies that indicate that church people are much more prone to being overweight. If you doubt the statistics, take a sheet of paper to your next church service and make a mark on your sheet of paper for every obese person you see. You will be astounded at the number of your count.

A Southern Baptist publication stated, *"A new study recently published by Purdue University Professor Ken*

Ferraro examined the relationships between religion and both body mass index (BMI) and obesity. The study found that church members tend to be more overweight than the general population, and Baptists, including Southern Baptists, have the distinction of being the most overweight religious group in the study." [13]

A study conducted by Matthew Feinstein which included over 2,400 people tracked for 18 years, concluded that people who regularly attend church are 50% more likely to be obese by the time they reach middle age. Christians are quick to condemn those addicted to alcohol, drugs, pornography, but they don't seem to recognize or realize that overeating is also an addiction. The Binge Eating Disorder (BED) has actually been the subject of scientific studies. We are most familiar with the terms of anorexia and bulimia, but food can be an addiction without either of these extremes.

Food addiction could be driven by anxiety. If we are emotionally upset, anxious, or fearful, we eat food to make ourselves feel better. That is an addictive connection as pertinent as drinking alcohol by an alcoholic. If we eat to make ourselves feel better, rather than submitting our fears or anxiety to God, we have made an idol out of our food.

Obesity is not necessarily connected to an addictive drive. It could be that my bodily appetite is simply out of line. I enjoy gorging myself. That is what the Bible describes as gluttony. I Corinthians 10:31 asserts, *"So whether you eat or drink whatever you do, do it all for the glory of God."* It is obvious that our appetite for food should be under the control of our wills and not subject to our bodily desires. Obesity also leads our bodies into numerous diseases such as heart failure and diabetes. It has also been linked certain types of cancer. We must control our bodily appetites!

So Which Sin is the Worst

Romans 6:23 says, *"For the wages of sin is death."* I Corinthians 6:9-11 states, *"Or do you not know that wrongdoers will not inherit the kingdom of God? Do not be deceived: neither the sexually immoral nor idolaters nor adulterers nor men who have sex with men nor thieves nor the greedy nor drunkards nor slanders nor swindlers will inherit the kingdom of God. And that is what some of you were. But you were washed, you were sanctified, you were justified in the name of the Lord Jesus Christ and by the spirit of our God."* It is obvious from this list that sin is sin. Every Christian, like me, should desire to be on the past tense part of this sin list, *"that is what some of you were."* Any disobedience to God's commandments or principles is sin and brings death and separation from God. Jesus said in John 14:15," *If you love me you will keep my commands."* So it really doesn't matter if it was the cookie I stole from grandma's cookie jar and lied about, or if I committed adultery. We are not to practice sin of any kind. John the beloved writes in I John 2:4-6, *"Whoever says, 'I know him,' but does not do what He commands is a liar, and the truth is not in that person. But if anyone obeys his word, love for God is truly made complete in them. This is how we know we are in him: whoever claims to live in him must live as Jesus did."*

So are we perfect as believers? Absolutely not! Which is why first I John 1:9 affirms, *"If we confess our sins, he is faithful and just and will forgive us our sins and purify us from all unrighteousness."* A true believer of Jesus Christ is putting off sin and learning to walk as Jesus did. We do not continually practice unrighteousness. If we do, we need to really ask ourselves if we have truly repented and believed the gospel. I John 3:6 says, *"No one who lives in him keeps on sinning* [some translations state this as "practicing sin"]. *No one who continues to sin has either seen him or known him."* Unfortunately there is a perverted grace movement in America. This movement erroneously declares that I can do any sin I want because I am in Christ. The scriptures I have already quoted make it very clear that this is a mistaken belief!

So what happens to us as believers if we continue to practice sin? The church is supposed to take action when someone is actively practicing sin. In I Corinthians 5:1-5, Paul is writing to the church on how to deal with a member practicing immorality. He plainly says," *It is actually reported that there is sexual immorality among you, and of a kind that even pagans do not tolerate: A man is sleeping with his father's wife. And you are proud! Shouldn't you rather have gone into mourning and have put out of your fellowship the man who has been doing this? For my part, even though I am not physically present, I am with you in spirit. As one who is present with you in this way, I have already passed judgment in the name of our Lord Jesus on the one who has been doing this. So when you are assembled and I am with you in spirit, and the power of our Lord Jesus is present, hand this man over to Satan for the destruction of the flesh, so that his spirit may be saved on the day of the Lord."*

This is not to be done in a vitriolic manner. Matthew 18 describes the three steps we are to take in this matter. In love we are to privately approach and rebuke a brother or sister practicing sin to attempt to bring them to repentance. If they refuse private confrontation, then we are to take two more witnesses. If they refuse to repent in front of the witnesses, then we are to take them to the "assembly" or church. If they are unwilling to repent, the option is clear-*"hand this man* [or woman] *over to Satan for the destruction of the flesh, so that his spirit may be saved on the day of the Lord."* First John chapter 5:16 states: *"If you see any brother or sister commit a sin that does not lead to death, you should pray and God will give them life. I refer to those whose sin does not lead to death. There is a sin that leads to death. I am not saying that you should pray about that."* It should be obvious that loving church discipline is delivering a brother or sister who does not repent from ongoing sin to the destroyer. I have never witnessed this in any church I ever attended, yet it seems an obvious directive when someone refuses to repent after having been lovingly confronted. In the book of II Corinthians we actually discover that this man, for whom Paul recommended church discipline, repented. This is the point of all church discipline, to bring people to repentance. The modern church is not practicing this in a loving and compassionate manner.

Part of our failure as the Church of Jesus Christ is our lack of making disciples. We have also not created a church atmosphere where people are safe to disclose their struggles. Screaming, ranting, and raving from the pulpit about sin that our denomination condemns does not create an atmosphere where people are safe to disclose their struggles. Their fear of rejection after disclosing the sin has kept believers captive to their sin. We must figure out how to be a friend of the sinners and tax collectors as Jesus was, and help people to be real, transparent, and destroy their religious masks.

Footnotes/Quotes

[1] [http://www.adherents.com/largecom/baptist_divorce.html]

[2] –See more at: http://www.childtrends.org/?indicators=births-to-un-married women#sthash.zf5Lj0Uc.dpuf

[3] http://www.focusonthefamily.com/marriage/divorce-and-infidelity/pornography-and-virtual-infidelity/virtual-infidelity-and-marriage

[4] *(http://www.expastors.com/how-many-pastors- are-addicted-to-porn-the-stats-are-surprising/).*

[5] *(http://www.stateofdatingreport.com/findings.htm).*

[6] [Read more at http://www.relevantmagazine.com/life/relation-ship/features/28337-the-secret-sexual-revolution#zKDtiaAZc-5SUy7Lg.99]

[7] *[http://www.todayschristianwoman.com/articles/2008/september/why-affairs-happen.html]*

[8] (http://www.pewresearch.org/fact-tank/2014/09/25/new-study-finds-a-greater-church-acceptance-of-gays-and-lesbians-2/)

[9] (http://www.pewresearch.org/fact-tank/2015/12/18/most-u-s-christian-groups-grow-more-accepting-of-homosexuality/)

[10] *http://thinkprogress.org/lgbt/2016/05/18/3779705/united-methodist-church-has-a-new-method/*

[11] *https://en.wikipedia.org/wiki/LGBT_clergy_in_Christianity*

[12] http://reverbpress.com/religion/abortion-rates-high-est-among-christians-according-stunning-survey-results/

[13] *http://www.sbclife.net/Articles/2007/01/sla8*

CHAPTER 4

LOVE OF MONEY AS IDOLATRY AND IDENTITY

I think one of the major idolatrous things that we worship in our western culture is our love of money. We will discuss how this applies to the church in another chapter. This chapter is about American families. Paul warned us in *I Timothy 6:10, "For the love of money is a root of all kinds of evil. Some people, eager for money, have wandered from the faith and pierced themselves with many griefs."* The writer of Hebrews warns us in chapter *13:5 "Keep your lives free from the love of money and be content with what you have, because God has said, 'Never will I leave you never will I forsake you.'"*

According to "new Gallup metrics," (http://www.gallup.com/poll/166211/worldwide-median-household-income-000.aspx) America is in the top six wealthiest countries in the world. Our median income is $43,585. Our median per capita income is $15,480. Liberia, one of the poorest countries in the world, has a median income of $781 and a median per capita income of $118. One of the constant rebukes to Israel in the Old Testament was their greediness. They used unjust weights and measures, deprived widows and orphans of their inheritances, and indulged themselves in feasts, orgies, and drunkenness. Isaiah 10:1-3 says, " *Woe to those who make unjust laws, to those who issue oppressive decrees, to deprive the poor of their rights and withhold justice from the oppressed of my people, making widows their prey and robbing the fatherless. What will you do on the day of reckoning, when disaster comes from afar? To whom will you run for help? Where will you leave your riches?*" Yet what we hear in America is a cry for more money and more wealth when we are one of the most prosperous nations in the world.

Prior to the middle 1800's, most families were agrarian in nature. People made their living by cultivating the land, and families also forged strong family connections as they worked together. The industrial revolution began to change the way western people made their livings, but it wasn't until after World War II that society was more deeply influenced by the industrial revolution. During WWII, women were drafted into the workforce because of the deployment of men and the lack of workers to produce wartime products needed to conquer the Nazi and Japanese forces. After WWII ended, women didn't want to go home and assume their old roles of mothering children and being homemakers. A major cultural shift happened. Between 1940 and 1945, the female percentage of the U.S. workforce increased from 27 percent to nearly 37 percent, and by 1945, nearly one out of every four married women worked outside the home. In our modern day culture, it is almost a necessity for both married partners to have employment to make a living.

People also began moving out of cities into suburbs during the transition time after World War II. Previously the rich had moved out of the cities, but now a new class of people was rising up. We now call them the middle class. These folks began to settle in single-family houses. They spread out buying lots of what was previously farmland next to the cities. Moving out of the city also created a huge need for transportation to get to work. People who formerly walked to work had to buy automobiles. Families where a wife and husband both worked had to buy two automobiles. Paying the mortgage, paying for automobiles, and putting gasoline in the cars created a huge monetary stress. During this time period, people also decided that large families were a bigger financial stress. Elements of birth control, abortion, and other means of limiting family size began to be discussed and applied, like illegal abortions. By the 1960s, the idealistic middle-class life included a house in the suburbs, two cars, an average of two or three children per household, and a pet.

However, the "hippie" generation of the 1960s rejected their parents middle-class values and the values of World War II and Korean veterans. A cultural discontentment with the Vietnam conflict initiated a protest movement. Verbally and physically rejecting their parent's values, hippies and protesters came up with sayings like:

- Make love not war. ~ Anonymous Hippie Quote
- Drop acid [LSD/drug] not bombs.~ Anonymous Hippie Quote

- Herb [marijuana] is the healing of a nation, alcohol is the destruction.~ Bob Marley
- If everyone demanded peace instead of another television set, then there would be peace.~ John Lennon
- F*ck the establishment.~ Anonymous Hippie Quote

These quotes from the '60s make it very clear how young people were rejecting their parents' so-called middle class values. Hippies founded their own counter-culture based on psychedelic rock music, LSD, and marijuana, and a sexual revolution despising marriage and embracing immorality, especially for young women. Communal living without marriage relationships was a hallmark of this retreat from their parent's middle class values and the suburbs of America.

In addition to the hippie's rejection of their parents' middle class values, in the 1960s we also saw the rise of President Lyndon B Johnson's "Great Society." One of the major mistakes of this policy was to offer money for family support if a father was not in the home. At first, needy families hid the male spouse. As this policy progressed in our culture, eventually women did not bother to get married. This stipend for having children out of wedlock has also helped us create a fatherless generation. This is one of the reasons many of our children are struggling with their sexual identities. Both male and female influences are important to healthy child development, but we have reared a generation of orphaned children with living parents.

So how has our love of money "pierced us with griefs" as Paul warned? An entire generation rejected their parents values because of our love of money. The present millennial generation seems to have developed an attitude of entitlement directed towards parents and our government. The moral impact that this "Hippie counterculture" had on our society is still being felt today. Prior to the 1960s, America had a moral base founded on our exposure to Christian values. At this point our culture seems to be morally valueless.

Prior to the 1960s, America had a moral base founded on our exposure to Christian values and revivals. At age 55, I was working on a counseling degree at Regent University in Virginia Beach, Virginia. I had a classmate who was my age, but we were brought up in two very different environments in the 1950s. I was reared in Michigan on a farm and I was white. She was reared in Virginia in the inner city and was an African-American. One day I initiated a conversation with my classmate about moral values and what we experienced growing up. What we discovered was that the moral values of farmers in the rural north and the southern, inner-city values were almost identical. We discussed divorce, alcoholism, drug addiction, out of wedlock pregnancies, abandonment of family members, and other moral issues. What we discovered together is that our communities disapproved and shunned any person who was breaking moral law based on God's word. This morality in non-Christian environments was the result of previous revivals. Would to God that the morals that reigned in our society then were still in place now. Whether or not people were believers, they were still living by Biblical principles. Now not even believers are living by Biblical principles. We Christians represent a rebellious, arrogant, stubborn, stiff-necked nation, rebelling against the God of heaven. We must repent.

CHAPTER 5

TIME WASTERS AS IDOLATRY

Do you understand what the word "amusement" means? Most dictionaries agree that it comes from an old French word "_amuser_" which meant, *"to stupefy, waste time, be lost in thought."* I personally am wondering if the application of the Greek/Latin approach to the word is more appropriate. Using this approach, the prefix *"a"* would be a negative with the meaning *"not."* The root word *"muse,"* would have the meaning *"to think."* Using this approach to the word we have the definition, *"not to think."* I think this goes hand-in-hand with the French definition, *"to stupefy, waste time, be lost in thought."* I'm going to ruffle some more feathers by pointing out some American traditions that are amusements, or time wasters, distracting our brains from what is really important.

So why am I concentrating on "Time Wasters" as a subject? I run discipleship groups for Christian men who are struggling to break free from addictions. It is absolutely astounding to me what a major problem it is for these men to find 15 minutes a day to spend cultivating a relationship with God. As the men begin to put aside this time to cultivate a relationship with their heavenly Father, they begin to develop their identity based on that relationship. They begin to find increasing victory over their addiction. Jesus said, " *My sheep listen to my voice; I know them, and they follow me.*"(John 10:27) It is of major importance that we as believers spend time with the Lord on a daily basis, reading the word, praying, and quieting ourselves to listen to Him. This is why I am addressing subjects that steal our time.

Bowing to a Television

The first time waster I want to address is our television viewing habits. Here are the statistics from a 204cNielsen report clarifying the amount of time by age group that Americans spend watching television. "*The Nielsen report suggests that our media habits have remained fairly steady over the last few years, though smartphone usage and time-shifted television are growing...Specifically, says Nielsen, here's the average weekly usage* [television viewing] *for ascending age groups:*
age 2-11: 24 hours, 16 minutes;
age 12-17: 20 hours, 41 minutes;
age 18-24: 22 hours, 27 minutes;
age 25-34: 27 hours, 36 minutes;
age 35-49: 33 hours, 40 minutes;
age 50-64: 43 hours, 56 minutes;
age 65-plus: 50 hours, 34 minutes." '

I am not posing an attack against children's programs, educational shows, cooking shows, sports broadcasts (unless they include semi-nude cheerleaders), or family oriented shows. What I do want to point out for your consideration, is that the general content of prime time television in the year 2016 would have been considered pornography in 1960. Regardless of our age we are all exposed to acts of violence, homosexuality or lesbianism, sexual innuendo, and this is no longer limited to HBO or other specialty channels. Major broadcasting companies are increasing sexual acts, murders, violence, and nudity in the shows that are televised before 9PM when children are still viewing programming. Children are not my only concern with the increase of carnality in television broadcasting. When we expose our minds as adults to things that are sinful and carnal, we are opening ourselves up to deception. James warns us in his epistle in chapter 1:21-22, "*Therefore, get rid of all moral filth and the evil that is so prevalent and humbly accept the word planted in you, which can save you. Do not merely listen to the word, and so deceive yourselves. Do what it says.*" The moral filth and evil is flooding television networks. Adults should not think they are immune to this evil.

Here is a study that is four years old that was done on nudity in broadcast television. The study was posted by Fox news. "*The Parents Television Council (PTC), a nonprofit organization dedicated to educating parents about television content, has released a new study looking at nudity on prime-time broadcast television which reveals a major increase over the 2011-2012 season. The study found that there were 76 incidents of full nudity on 37 shows compared to 15 incidents in 14 shows the previous ratings season, representing a 407 percent rise in incidents. Almost 70 percent of the scenes that featured such nudity were on shows which aired prior to 9pm, compared to 50 percent of the full nudity scenes which aired before 9pm during the 2010-2011 season. In addition, the study says only five of the 76 full-nudity depictions contained an "S" descriptor to warn parents to the explicit nature of the episode. But perhaps the most jaw-dropping finding was in regard to full-frontal nudity. While just one incidence of this occurred during the 2010-2011 study period, 64 documented full-frontal incidences occurred this past season, a 6,300 percent increase. CBS and FOX declined to comment on the study, and ABC, CW and NBC – all of which had programs mentioned in the study – did not respond to a request for comment. In addition, the FCC did not respond for comment."* [2]

Here is another article published online by Mr. Tim Winter, "*Why has TV gotten worse?*" He states, *"It's not that times have changed. The problem lies with the TV content ratings system and the people who were appointed to ensure that the system is accurate. The ratings system was originally created by Congress as part of the Telecommunications Act of 1996, to give parents tools to protect their children from harmful TV content. Implementation of the system was done by the TV industry. But the dirty secret is that the ratings system has provided cover for the TV industry – allowing TV content to become more graphic, more explicit, and more adult over time. As soon as America got the V-chip, which utilizes an accurate ratings system to block unwanted content, Americans also got some of the most offensive and indecent programming on television. The V-chip, coupled with the ratings system, has allowed those who have wanted to push the envelope to do so – all the while dumping the responsibility for protecting children solely on parents. We analyzed the past 20 years of the TV content ratings system, and found widespread, systemic problems that render the system inadequate for protecting children from graphic sex, violence, and profanity on television. Our new research found there are fewer programs on prime-time broadcast television rated TV-PG, and there are fewer differences between the content of programs rated TV-PG and those rated TV-14. Even worse, graphic TV content has increased in both amount and intensity and yet all content on broadcast TV is rated as appropriate for a 14-year-old child or younger. Additionally, there are no TV-MA rated (the highest adult TV rating) shows on broadcast TV. It's not that some of the shows don't warrant the MA rating, it's that the networks are finan- cially motivated not to rate programs properly because most corporate sponsors won't advertise on MA-rated programs."* [3]

The apostle Paul warns us about exposing our minds to things that are improper, and that includes adults not just our children. He warns us that we are to guard our minds. In Ephesians chapter 4:17-24, we read this exhor- tation: *"So I tell you this, and insist on it in the Lord, that you must no longer live as the Gentiles do, in the futility of their thinking. They are darkened in their understanding and separated from the life of God because of the igno- rance that is in them due to the hardening of their hearts. Having lost all sensitivity, they have given themselves over to sensuality so as to indulge in every kind of impu- rity, and they are full of greed. That, however, is not the way of life you learned when you heard about Christ and were taught in him in accordance with the truth that is in Jesus. You were taught, with regard to your former way of life, to put off your old self, which is being corrupted by its deceitful desires; to be made new in the attitude of your minds; and to put on the new self, created to be like God in true righteousness and holiness."* It is our responsibility as believers in Jesus Christ to guard not only what comes into our minds, but to guard what our children are exposed to in our homes. The general content of broadcast television is indecent and should be avoided by Christian families. Someone may assert, "I watch broadcast television, and it doesn't bother me." Perhaps you should consider if you have lost your sensitivity and have given your mind over to sensuality.

Computers and Cell Phones as Time Wasters

In my work with addicts, some men have acknowledged spending over 12 hours a day playing computer games. They have become dependent on other people to feed and house them. A phenomena that we are experiencing in our nation is the number of young people that are returning to parental homes in their 20s expecting their parents to care for them rather than making a living for themselves. The apostle Paul is very clear about taking responsibility for ourselves. In II Thessalonians 3:6-10, he gives us this commandment: *"In the name of the Lord Jesus Christ, we command you, brothers and sisters, to keep away from every believer who is idle and disruptive and does not live according to the teaching you received from us. For you yourselves know how you ought to follow our example. We were not idle when we were with you, nor did we eat anyone's food without paying for it. On the contrary, we worked night and day, laboring and toiling so that we would not be a burden to any of you. We did this, not because we do not have the right to such help, but in order to offer ourselves as a model for you to imitate. For even when we were with you, we gave you this rule: "The one who is unwilling to work shall not eat."* "

The next statistic I quote does not contradict the television age statistics quoted earlier. This is a general population statistic, and covers all age groups. "*In the United States, people spend an average of 444 minutes every day looking at screens, or 7.4 hours. That breaks down to 147 minutes spent watching TV, 103 minutes in front of a computer, 151 minutes on a smartphones and 43 minutes with a tablet.*"[4] Comparing this with the television watching hours, we should keep in mind that it is extremely unlikely that older Americans own all of these devices. The younger the age group, the more likely it is that they own multiple screened devices. Senior citizens over the age of 65, might own a cell phone and a television. Those in the age span of 50-65, most likely own a computer, cell phone, and a television. Those under the age of 50 are more likely to own all of the mentioned devices.

The next statistic focuses on teenagers. "*According to a recent study by Yahoo! In collaboration with Carat Interactive, American teenagers and young people aged 13 to 24 spend an average of 16.7 hours online every week, excluding email time.*"[5] Are you beginning to get the idea that electronic devices captivate a great deal of our time and attention? When we consider the aforementioned breakdowns in the American family, *("Fewer than half (46%) of U.S. kids younger than 18 years of age are living in a home with two married heterosexual parents in their first marriage. This is a marked change from 1960, when 73% of children fit this description, and 1980, when 61% did...")* it should not surprise us that our children are dealing with major rejection issues. I believe that the increase in the "sexting," cyberbullying, and attempting to connect with online conversations has to do with our children's fear of developing a real, face-to-face relationship, and also our failure to make disciples. Human beings were created for relationship. God said, *"it is not good for man to be alone..."(Gen. 2:18)*. Texting someone on a cell phone or on a computer does not take any relational skills. In my opinion, we have reared an orphaned generation with living parents who have isolated themselves and use electronic equipment to replace relationships.

James 1:27 asserts, *"Religion that God our Father accepts as pure and faultless is this: to look after orphans and widows in their distress and to keep oneself from being polluted by the world."* The first way we accomplish this as the body of Christ is by making disciples. The second way we accomplish this is by fathering the fatherless while keeping ourselves pure and unpolluted by the world. With the present state of immorality among men in the Christian church, this is almost an impossibility. With almost 70% of church men involved in pornography, it is hard to ask any male to safely visit a widow. Those of us who are walking in purity, have an obligation to fulfill this directive and father the fatherless while teaching them how to have a relationship with Father God.

So let me ask you a very pertinent question-how much time per day do you spend cultivating a relationship with God? As you compare this time to your amusements, are you actually bowing to an idol in some form? I think our own personal time with God is very important. I also think that prayer with our spouse is very important. And the scripture commands us to teach our children the Word of God. Age appropriate songs, Bible stories, Biblical radio or television for children, and family devotions are very important in this process. So are you and your family invested in the Word of God? As you compare the amount of time spent by your family on amusements to the time you have invested in spiritual endeavors, are you worshiping an idol that is called "amusement?"

Footnotes/Sources

[1] *http://www.nydailynews.com/life-style/ average-american-watches-5-hours-tv-day-article-1.1711954*

[2] *http://www.foxnews.com/entertainment/2012/08/23/new-study-says-full-frontal-nudity-on-prime-time-tv-up-400-over-last-year. html*

[3] *http://www.breitbart.com/big-hollywood/2016/04/28/why-tv-content-has-gotten-worse-cable-networks-control-parental-guide-lines-system/*

[4] *http://bgr.com/2014/05/29/ smartphone-computer-usage-study-chart/*

[5] *https://www.reference.com/family/much-time-american-teenag-ers-spend-computers-day-ee401fc863e147ad*

CHAPTER 6

DIVISION IN THE CHURCH AS GOD MOVES

Here is the bottom line of this chapter upfront: Whenever God begins a movement among His people, we can expect things that our religion or denomination does not endorse. This usually brings division rather than unification because we are so engrossed with our religious traditions. Believing denominational leaders need to repent publicly to each other for condemning those in other denominations who are truly following Jesus after further movements, revivals, and awakenings of the Holy Spirit. Bible believing Christians can have doctrinal differences and denominational preferences, but scripture does not give us the right to condemn or vilify those who disagree with our beliefs. The apostle Paul commanded us in Philippians 2:3, *"Do nothing out of rivalry or conceit, but in humility consider others as more important than yourselves."* What would our religious culture actually look like if we applied this verse to other denominations? Paul then explains how our Savior laid aside the splendor and majesty of Heaven to take on human flesh and give up His life to atone for our sins. We must present a true characteristic of loving one another between Bible-believing denominations. Division and hatred does not impress unbelievers or impress God. What would our nation look like if all denominational rivalry was put aside?

I have the personal privilege of belonging to a church that is multiethnic on purpose. I am a member of New Life Church, in the Tidewater area of Virginia. Pastor Dan Backens, a white, farm-reared, country boy from Idaho, and Pastor Kevin Turpin, an African-American boy from Southampton, New York, founded the church in 1999. While these two men were working on their advanced degrees at Regent University and in fellowship while employed at a local church, they began to discuss what it might look like to establish a church that could minister to multiple ethnic groups. They launched their plan and they were successful! At this point at least half of our church is racially mixed. Our church includes Hispanic members, African-American members, Asian American members, white members, and numerous other ethnic groups from around the world. Pastor Dan and Kevin's Church plant had a humble beginning of several hundred people, but is now a mega church with over 3000+ members, three different campuses, nine weekly services, and a multiethnic staff. So how did they make this church plant successful? Glad you asked! Here are parts of the story from my viewpoint based on some of their public explanations.

Pastor Dan had a liturgical, Lutheran background, but came to know the Lord at a "home group" type meeting while he was in college. This home group was part of what we now call the "Jesus People" revival of the 1960s and early 70s. Pastor Kevin came from a Baptist-Pentecostal background. I believe the first wise thing they did in launching a multiethnic church was not branding the church with a denominational label. The second wise thing they did was to declare the church as Charismatic not Pentecostal. This confirmed that they believed that all of the gifts of Spirit were operational, but distanced themselves from some "required" behaviors in the Pentecostal church, which were enacted to "prove" that you were spiritual. The third thing they did incorporated contemporary Christian songs within an African-American style of worship. This allowed them to meld both blacks and whites in the worship service. This did not cater to the older folks who grew up with traditional African-American or white music, hymns, gospel songs, and choir anthems, or well-polished soloists. This did provide a modern, contemporary atmosphere where people could lay aside previous denominational preferences, styles of worship, and the church "performance" modes of traditional behaviors that seemingly asserted spirituality. This atmosphere continues to be a burgeoning place of prayer, evangelism, missionary endeavors, ministries to the poor, jail ministries, feeding the homeless, providing tutors for children in public schools, ministering to addicts, and reaching a younger generation for Christ in a multiethnic, trans-denominational atmosphere. They were and are successful!

Do all churches need to look like the New Life Church-absolutely not! But their approach and their plan could be used by anyone in any city or ethnically diverse country area to create a multiethnic church. Division does not represent Jesus' heart or the Father's heart for the body of Christ. Jesus prayed a very specific prayer of unity for His disciples and those who would follow in their steps. In John chapter 17:9-23, we read: *"I pray for them. I am not praying for the world, but for those you have given me, for they are yours. All I have is yours, and all you have is mine. And glory has come to me through them. I will remain in the world no longer, but they are still in the world, and I am coming to you. Holy Father, protect them by the power of your name, the name you gave me, so that they may be one as we are one. My prayer is not for them alone. I pray also for those who will believe in me through their message, that all of them may be one, Father, just as you are in me and I am in you. May they also be in us so that the world may believe that you have sent me. I have given them the glory that you gave me, that they may be one as we are one — I in them and you in me — so that they may be brought to complete unity. Then the world will know that you sent me and have loved them even as you have loved me."* So does anyone think that the believing church in America is walking in complete unity as Jesus prayed?

Jesus' greatest enemy was religion. Those who tried to take His life and persecuted Him when He was alive were the religious leaders of the Jews. The reason they persecuted Him, was not because He did not honor the Word of God, but because He did not keep the religious traditions of the Jews. You may recall the Jews condemned Jesus' disciples for eating with unwashed hands, which was against Jewish *tradition*. It was not a command from the Law of God. In Mark chapter 7:8-13, after this accusation by the Pharisees, Jesus directly addresses the problem of following the traditions of men: *"...You have let go of the commands of God and are holding on to human traditions. And He continued, "You have a fine way of setting aside the commands of God in order to observe your own traditions! For Moses said, 'Honor your father and mother,' and, 'Anyone who curses their father or mother is to be put to death.' But you say that if anyone declares that what might have been used to help their father or mother is Corban (that is, devoted to God)—then you no longer let them do anything for their father or mother. Thus you nullify the word of God by your tradition that you have handed down. And you do many things like that."*

Unfortunately Jesus has a new "traditional" enemy in our current age, denominational labels and traditions. Almost without exception most denominational labels are monuments to past reformations or revivals. To our shame many pastors and believers use past moves of God to denounce and repudiate other moves of God rather than rejoicing and joining in when God births a new movement or restores something missing to the church.

We should be able to rejoice that Martin Luther restored to the church the principle that salvation comes through faith and God's grace. We should be able to rejoice that John Calvin restored sound Biblical teaching to the church. We should celebrate that the Lutheran pastor, P. J. Spener, launched the movement of Pietism by emphasizing Bible reading and prayer when Lutheranism was becoming cold and dead. We should take great joy in the 24-7 prayer movement launched by Pietist, Count Nikolaus Ludwig von Zinzendorf who sheltered differing faith refugees from Catholic persecution. He united them around Holy Communion and launched the missionary movement and prayer movement that continues influencing 24-7 prayer movements all over the world. We should rejoice that the Quaker movement, birthed in the middle 1600s, which blessed the ministry of women and emphasized hearing the Lord's voice. We should take great joy that the Wesleyan revival turned Britain into a flaming Christian nation from cold, dead, Anglican (reformed political Catholicism) religion. We should be grateful that Jonathan Edwards and George Whitefield, influenced by the Wesley's, led the first great awakening in the American colonies and motivated further missionary works to the American Indians and African-Americans held in slavery. We should also be grateful that their great awakening evangelized slaves. John Wesley's condemnation of slavery led to the ordination of African-American pastors in America and began a movement, especially in the northern states, that would eventually lead to the civil war and freeing the slaves. Our hearts should rejoice over the Baptist and Methodist circuit-riding preachers that evangelized the colonies and states as our nation was being birthed and formed churches in the wilderness for settlers. We should take great delight in the second great awakening at the Cain Ridge revival birthed by a Methodist lay preacher as settlers gathered for Holy Communion. We should shout for joy that the restoration of charismatic gifting to the church actually began in Ohio with Maria Woodworth Etter as she saw many divine healings as she began to pray for the sick in 1885. People also spoke in tongues in Maria's meetings and were heard in known languages like Hebrew and Arabic. When unbelievers in the congregation heard their own languages they were converted to Jesus. John Alexander Dowie was also experiencing divine healings across the state of California in 1888. This preceded the Azusa Street revival by 21 years. We should rejoice and be grieved by the Azusa Street revival which God intended to be a racial reconciliation. The revival was led by Charles Parham, William Seymour, Frank Bartleman, and William Durham. Unfortunately what began as an African-American and white revival with Chinese and Mexican participants ended in further racial division rather than reconciliation. Fortunately this revival led to a further missionary outpouring that began to cover the world evangelizing Asian, African, and South American countries.

The 20th Century saw various moves of God and revivals throughout the United States. John G. Lake's healing rooms in Spokane, Washington, we're founded in 1914 as a result of the Azusa Street Pentecostal outpouring. After the Azusa outpouring, 20th century ministries were birthed by: Aimee Semple McPherson, Florence Crawford, A. H. Argue, R. E. McAlister, A. C. Valdez, Carrie Judd Montgomery, Charles Price, Raymond T. Richey, and a host of others in America. Over ninety evangelists birthed the second wave of the 20th Century healing revival in the 40s and 50s. Some of the most well-known healing evangelists were: Jack Coe, A. A. Allen, T. L. Osborn, W. V. Grant, Don Stewart, Kathryn Kuhlman and Morris Cerullo. This outpouring was followed by the Jesus People Movement, that occurred during the hippie movement of the 1960s and early 1970s, which also birthed contemporary praise and worship music. Let us not forget the charismatic renewal in the Catholic Church and other liturgical churches in the 1970s. The next great outpouring in North America was the Toronto, Canada, revival of 1994, and the Pensacola, Florida, revival of 1995. John and Carol Arnott birthed the Toronto revival in the Toronto Vineyard as they invited Randy Clark to minister at their church. The Brownsville revival was fathered by pastor John Kilpatrick and was ushered in by evangelist Steve Hill. Millions of people from around the world visited these revivals taking the anointing back to their own countries and churches.

Many of these revivals were accompanied by phenomena that could not be humanly explained. I am not referring only to divine healings or speaking in tongues, which characterized the Pentecostal revival. The Pietists and Quakers received words from the Lord preceding the modern prophetic movement. John Wesley's conversion occurred after his brother Charles was miraculously healed after a prophetic word by a young girl from Zinzendorf's influence. At John Wesley's outdoor meetings people had to be warned not to climb into trees to get a better view of the evangelist because they were falling out of the trees unconscious under the power of God and were injured. This preceded the modern pentecostal phenomena of being "slain in the Spirit." If you read Wesley's journal, you will find that demonized people were delivered. This also did not match the theology of the day. As Jonathan Edwards read his manuscript, *Sinners in the Hands of an Angry God,* in a calm level voice, people screamed and fell to the floor unconscious. Some of them were unconscious for several days. This also did not match the Reformed theology of the day. Whenever God begins a movement among His people, we can expect things that our religion or denomination does not endorse. This usually brings division rather than unification because we are so engrossed with our religious traditions.

Examples of the divisions are easily seen in each of these movements. Martin Luther was excommunicated from the Roman Catholic Church. The Reformation also spawned religiously based wars. John Wesley and his brother Charles were kicked out of the Anglican Church when he began to preach and teach with passion and fire. This led to the founding of the Methodist denomination which still has Anglican traditions. Jonathan Edwards did not escape unscathed from the first great awakening. In 1741 Edwards published <u>The Distinguishing Marks of a Work of the Spirit of God</u>, dealing particularly with the phenomena most criticized: the swoonings, outcries, and convulsions. In 1749 Jonathan Edwards was voted out of the church. Maria Woodworth Etters earliest connection was with the Disciples of Christ. They did not accept women in ministry and forbid her to preach. She began to associate with Quakers where she received her baptism in the Holy Spirit. She associated with the Brethren in Christ for a short period of time, and then joined the (pre-pentecostal) Church of God of General Eldership. She was dismissed from their denomination in 1904. So what am I pointing out here? Whenever God moves within a denominational structure and does something empowered by the Spirit of God, people react negatively because of religious traditions. It is an honorable thing to honor those who ushered in previous moves of God, but it is a dishonorable thing to condemn and curse present moves of God that do not match our denominational history.

It should be plain that these movements of God brought millions of people into the kingdom of God, healed the sick, delivered people from demonic oppression, raised the dead, restored families, saved nations from revolutions, broke the chains of slavery, and set the captives free. So why do we always see religious traditions rebelling against every move of God? I believe it is because religious tradition is Jesus's greatest enemy.

We have the same problem in our present church society. I have spoken with brothers and sisters in Christ who have had pastors tell them if they joined another denomination they would go to hell. How does this represent the oneness in Christ's love and the love that Jesus prayed that we should have? It does not! I am not referring to the liberal attempt to unify the church from something other than God's word. What if we could unify around the basic Christian doctrines as found in the apostles Creed? Here is the apostles Creed to remind you of the basic tenets of Christianity:

I believe in God, the Father almighty,
creator of heaven and earth;
I believe in Jesus Christ, His only Son, our Lord.
He was conceived by the power of the Holy Spirit
and born of the Virgin Mary.
He suffered under Pontius Pilate,
was crucified, died, and was buried.
He descended to the dead.
On the third day He rose again.
He ascended into heaven,
and is seated at the right hand of the Father.
He will come again to judge the living and the dead.

**I believe in the Holy Spirit,
the holy catholic [universal] Church,
the communion of saints,
the forgiveness of sins
the resurrection of the body,
and the life everlasting. Amen.**

If anyone actually believes and follows these basic tenants and has accepted Jesus' sacrifice for our sins by faith, they are our brother or sister. What if we could honor every new move of God and test the spirits to see if they were of God? Would that not be following the commands of God's word? Would we not be embracing what God is doing in the world rather than rejecting and criticizing restorative moves of God?

The Vineyard Church excluded the Toronto Vineyard as the revival broke out in 1994. They were afraid of the manifestations that were occurring in the meetings. They later repented and asked forgiveness after breaking the fellowship. Asking forgiveness was a Godly thing to do. We need to follow their example and repent of the denominational condemnations that we state over other believing Christians. We need to unite around the truth of God's word, not around compromising His word, or condemning new moves of the Spirit of God. In my opinion, believing denominational leaders need to repent publicly to each other for condemning those who are following Jesus. Perhaps they should publicly wash one another's feet to illustrate their repentance and humility to one another.

We must repent of denominational divisions, unite ourselves around the truth of the Word of God and basic

Christian doctrine, and not be afraid when God does something new that violates our "religious traditions." We need to throw our traditions out the window and invite Father God to be the head of His church. If we were obedient to Father God and the moves of His Spirit, we would not be divided but unified. We would not be fearful of losing church members to another denomination. The apostle Paul gave us an exhortation in Ephesians chapter 4 that rebukes our denominational divisions. He said, "... *I urge you to live a life worthy of the calling you have received. Be completely humble and gentle; be patient, bearing with one another in love. Make every effort to keep the unity of the Spirit through the bond of peace. There is one body and one Spirit, just as you were called to one hope when you were called; one Lord, one faith, one baptism; one God and Father of all, who is over all and through all and in all."* Denominational divisions would not exist if we followed this exhortation.

Allow me to repeat the paragraph that introduced this chapter. Division does not represent Jesus' heart or the Father's heart for the body of Christ. Jesus prayed a very specific prayer of unity for his disciples and those who would follow in their steps. In John chapter 17:9-23, we read: *"I pray for them. I am not praying for the world, but for those you have given me, for they are yours. All I have is yours, and all you have is mine. And glory has come to me through them. I will remain in the world no longer, but they are still in the world, and I am coming to you. Holy Father, protect them by the power of your name, the name you gave me, so that they may be one as we are one. My prayer is not for them alone. I pray also for those who will believe in me through their message, that all of them*

72

may be one, Father, just as you are in me and I am in you. May they also be in us so that the world may believe that you have sent me. I have given them the glory that you gave me, that they may be one as we are one—I in them and you in me—so that they may be brought to complete unity. Then the world will know that you sent me and have loved them even as you have loved me."

CHAPTER 7

RACIAL DIVISION AND SEGREGATION IN AMERICA

One of the most racially divided places in America is our Sunday morning church services. I believe that one of the major causes of this division is, once again, our denominational and racial traditions. Doctor Martin Luther King Junior said in 1963, *"It is appalling that the most segregated hour of Christian America is 11 o'clock on Sunday morning..."* 11 o'clock was the time that most Christian services began, which is why he used that time as a reference. 54 years after his comment, in spite of the civil rights advances, the church remains overwhelmingly racially divided. Approximately 5 to 7.5 percent of churches in the U.S. are racially diverse, meaning that at least 20 percent of a church's members don't belong to the predominant racial group. Chris Rice, coauthor of <u>More Than Equals: Racial Healing for the Sake of the Gospel</u>, stated. *"Ninety percent of African-American*

Christians worship in all-black churches. Ninety percent of white American Christians worship in all-white churches...Years since the incredible victories of the civil rights movement, we continue to live in the trajectory of racial fragmentation. The biggest problem is that we don't see that as a problem."

An Overlooked Racial Division

When I speak of racial division, most Americans immediately think of divisions between African-Americans and white Americans. Though that is a problem that we will address, the worst racial division in America was and still is between Americans and the American Indians.

America, the new world, was not an uninhabited continent. From coast to coast, Indian tribes had settled throughout the United States probably having navigated the Bering Land Bridge in Alaska after the tower of Babel was destroyed. After Christopher Columbus' so called discovery of America, (Columbus thought he was in the country of India which is where the term "Indians" came from) Indian tribes began to have contact with Europeans. The Caribbean islands were the first to be overrun by settlers from Europe. The Europeans were armed with metallic weapons such as swords and gunpowder bearing armaments like cannons, and firearms. The Caribbean Islanders and Indian tribes of North America were no match for these metal weapons and gunpowder propelled firearms. The Caribbean Islanders were captured, enslaved, and many were deported to be sold as slaves in Europe. American Indians were also deported and sold as slaves. Those who remained on the islands became slaves for plantation owners who overtook their land. The situation was not much better in North America although it took more than a 100 years for the same impact to be experienced by Indian tribes in North America. If you doubt the truth of what I am stating, I invite you to read histories of the French Indian wars, the New York Indian wars, the Trail of Tears history, or the story of the Seminole war, <u>Hunted Like A Wolf</u> by Milton Meltzer.[1] You will be stunned by the atrocities committed by white Europeans on American Indians throughout our nation's early history and the multitude of treaties that we have broken.

Milton Meltzer in his book <u>Hunted Like a Wolf,</u> wrote the following about North American settlers: *"Among the baggage the white man carried with him to these shores was the belief that skin color made him superior. In his mind colored people were inferior to white. He identified the red man and the black man with evil, with savagery. It gave him an excuse for enslaving or killing Indians and blacks. Colored people were good only for doing the hard and dirty work the white man did not want to do."* This attitude dehumanized Indians and the African slaves. This allowed us an excuse to seize their land and use them as slaves.

This attitude did not characterize all settlers. There were good and Godly people from Europe who actually moved in with the Indian tribes to evangelize them. In 1787 chief Pachgantachilias said, *" I admit there are good white men, but they bear no proportion to the bad; the bad must be the strongest because they rule. They do what they please. They enslave those who are not of their color, although created by the same Great Spirit who created them. They would make slaves of us if they could; but as they cannot do it, they kill us. There is no Faith to be placed in their words."* This chiefs statement is a pretty good summation of non-Christian, racist viewpoints held by both Christians and non-believers alike regarding people of other skin colors.

Removal of the Cherokee Indians in 1838 from Georgia was the result of gold being discovered on Cherokee land. This forced relocation to lands west of the Mississippi River resulted in the death of thousands of Cherokee Indians through disease, hunger, and exposure to the winter elements. The only positive thing that happened during this tragedy was the fact that Christians took in and sheltered Cherokee refugees from the government. The California gold rush also led to the displacement of American Indian tribes, and Californians asked our government to make no treaties with the Indians. They simply displaced them with violence.

To the best of my knowledge and research, the United States of America made over 500 treaties with American Indians. My understanding is that not one of those treaties has been kept fully. If we claim as a Christian nation to serve a God who keeps His Word, then keeping our word to others to whom we have made promises should be important to us as believers. I do not have a clue how we as a nation begin to right the wrongs that we have done to the American Indian tribes. Scripture makes it clear that when we take something unjustly, we need to pay back with interest.

On October 21, 2016, numerous North American Indian tribes from America and Canada came together in Washington, DC to forgive Americans for the atrocities they committed against the Indian Nations. This gathering was organized by Reverend Negiel Bigpond, a fourth-generation evangelical pastor. This gathering had nothing to do with the American people repenting to the Indians. Pastor Bigpond stated, "We're going to receive the prayer of forgiveness from a nation that never asked to be forgiven. We feel that is more powerful." Prior to the assembly, he released a prayer that he intended to be used together at the gathering. The content is extraordinary. Here is the prayer: *"We the people, the host people of this great nation and the original lovers of this land, stand united with one heart and mind to bring the power of forgiveness to bear. As the host people of Turtle Island* [the Earth], *we forgive every atrocity and broken covenant ever designed to destroy us as a race of people. We break every curse, and renounce every lie, purposed to decimate us as human beings. We forgive the government, the church, and the educational system for the use of residential schools that attempted to destroy our culture and silence our voice as people by stealing our language.*

We stand in the gap for those who are unable or unwilling to forgive, and call upon the master of life to forgive us for harboring unforgiveness, resentment, hatred, bitterness and rage; We repent of every curse spoken over America by our ancestors and we release the power of forgiveness to bring healing and the peace of Creator God to this land. ... not returning evil for the evil perpetuated against us, but on the contrary we choose to release a blessing, knowing that the father of us all has called us as His children to bless and not curse, that we may inherit a blessing."

Lou Engle, a white man, also attended this prayer gathering in D.C. and spoke at the meeting. Lou Engle organized the 2016 "Azusa Now" prayer gathering and had a time of forgiveness and reconciliation with believing tribes of American Indians. The leaders also lead a time of tribal worship and dance at the gathering. Pastor Bigpond asserted one of his reasons for organizing the event was a statement made by Evangelist Billy Graham. In March of 1975, while speaking to a hundred Christian Indian leaders, Billy Graham asserted that the American Indian tribes will be a huge part of the next great revival or awakening in America. Pastor Bigpond is moving with the Tribes forward in faith. Revivals are already occurring on some reservations after the "Azusa Now" gathering. Now that the Indians have chosen to forgive our nation, perhaps some of our religious and political leaders can actually repent of the atrocities we committed against them.

Do you remember the story of Zacchaeus? After he took Jesus into his home, he repented of his sin and made this declaration: *"Look, Lord! Here and now I give half of my possessions to the poor, and if I have cheated anybody out of anything, I will pay back four times the amount." Jesus said to him, "Today salvation has come to this house, because this man, too, is a son of Abraham. For the Son of Man came to seek and to save the lost.""* (Luke 19:8-10) Did Jesus rebuke Zacchaeus for wanting to make his wrongs right? Absolutely not! He blessed him and asserted that, *"salvation has come to this house."* I'm not sure how we make things right with the American Indians, but it is obvious that we owe them for the land that we stole from them. Perhaps some of the billions of dollars that we spend on foreign aid should be directed towards American Indian tribes to right the wrongs we have committed.

White settlers traded alcohol to the Indians, gave them blankets with smallpox infections, murdered, poisoned, imprisoned, and massacred thousands of American Indians to get their land, the timber, animal skins for trading, and the gold, silver and other precious metals in their lands. It is obvious that we need to repent towards American Indian tribes, and ask our government officials to make these wrongs right. The first response, however, needs to come from the Church as we move in love and compassion to these estranged people groups stranded on reservations laden with poverty and addictions. Who is willing to take up this baton and run with it?

White and Black Historical Divisions

So where did this division originate that we now face between whites and blacks, and where do some of these traditions and prejudices come from? In my opinion Jim Crow laws endorsed after the Civil War continued the problem of segregation. Florida was the first state to endorse racial segregation politically after the Civil War. In 1887, Florida issued a series of regulations that required racial segregation in public transportation and other public facilities. By 1890, the South was fully segregated. Blacks had to drink from different water fountains from whites, use different bathrooms, and sit apart from whites in movie theaters, restaurants, and transportation. They attended separate schools and lived in separate neighborhoods. These laws made it difficult for African-Americans to hold church services. Blacks who violated these laws could be fined or jailed. If they could not pay the fines, they were required to perform forced labor to pay their fine. These "Jim Crow" laws recreated slavery-like conditions.

Prior to the Civil War, Christian slave owners in the south, and there were Christians slave owners, usually provided religious services for their slaves. These religious gatherings were separate from the white congregations. Slaves were allowed to go to services only after the slave owners were dressed, in their carriage, and on their way to their services. The lateness of the slave services also explains the necessity and frequency of fellowship meals after the African-American services. Eleven AM was a most common service time for white parishioners because it allowed farmers time to take care of the livestock and accomplish the morning chores before going to church.

This inculcation of Christianity in the South led to the conversion of many slaves to faith in Jesus Christ. Circuit riding preachers, especially the Methodists, also evangelized slaves and slave owners while preaching against the evils of slavery. Francis Asbury, a Methodist circuit-riding preacher, came to America in 1771. Asbury spent 45 years evangelizing numerous states on horseback and then by carriage when he could no longer sit on a horse. You may recall that John Wesley also traveled throughout Great Britain on horseback and preached against slavery. Asbury was merely imitating his mentor, John Wesley, although he was doing it in the frontier environment. Asbury was the head of the American Methodist Episcopal congregations.

In addition to the circuit riders who founded local congregations and ordained others into the pastorate, the Methodists and Baptists also held Camp meetings.

Awakenings broke out in the territories with settlers, particularly in the South, where Methodists found receptive people. These camp meetings led to several great awakenings or revivals throughout the frontier of the developing states of America. Crowds of up to 20,000 people attended camp meetings. That is astounding when we consider that their transportation was horse-driven or they arrived on foot. Camp meetings were held under tents or hastily built wooden shelters. These shelters usually covered only a portion of the attendees or musical instruments (pump organs) in use for the worship. The expectations Asbury placed upon himself and his Circuit riders produced fruit. In 1780, nine years after his arrival in America, there were 42 preachers and 8,504 members. Ten years later in 1790, there were 227 preachers and 45,949 white and 11,862 black members. In 1820, when Asbury passed away, there were 904 preachers and 256,881 members. When we consider the sparse populations of many of these frontier developments, which eventually became states, a quarter of a million believers is impressive! Prior to the Revolutionary war Virginia was evangelized by the same circuit riding Methodist preachers. Not only colonists and slaves came to Christ, but so did entire tribes of American Indians in the Virginia Beach area. These circuit-riding preachers had no racial boundaries that prevented them from preaching the gospel to all people! Would to God that this was the state of the body of Christ in our day-no racial boundaries!

The evangelization of slaves also gave us the wonderful tradition of what we now call "negro spirituals" which are rarely sung in church services anymore. The songs were made up by the slaves and often sung in the fields and in workplaces while slaves were laboring, in addition to being celebrated in worship services. Because of the hardships they were facing, many of these songs celebrated the idea of dying and going to heaven and receiving one's eternal reward from Jesus.

Because of the high illiteracy rate, and their poverty, the African-American congregations had no hymnals and few musical instruments. Worship leaders lined out new songs by singing a phrase and having the congregation repeat what they had sung. In modern times many African-American worship leaders still emulate this by improvising extra words or speak the words ahead of time before the congregation sings them. This is definitely tied to the old tradition of lining out songs, but many modern worship leaders have no idea where this "tradition" comes from. African-American musicians generally did not read music and made up their own harmonies. This differed greatly from white congregations. During the late 1800s and early 1900s, in white churches located in cities, congregations developed SATB choirs often accompanied by pipe organs in formal churches. This is a huge division in religious "traditions" and continues to divide white and black congregations between uneducated traditional and educated formal musicians.

Lining out hymns was not unique to African-American congregations. The American Puritans in the 1600s had no printing presses and also lined out hymns to teach their congregations Christian hymnody. But many of the Puritans were literate and had access to Bibles for their churches and a few hymnals for their worship leaders. The evangelization of the African-American community had taken place prior to the Civil War, but there were very few educated African-American pastors. The few African-American pastors who did have education and literacy were mostly located in the northern states. Many African-American preachers spoke what they had heard from white pastors or circuit riding preachers who had evangelized them. This repetition of what was heard and the music established an oral tradition in the African-American church which continues unconsciously today in many traditional African-American congregations.

Speaking of religious traditions, African-American congregations are also very verbal during the sermon. Congregants often made out loud comments such as: "Preach it brother! Amen! Come on. That's right! Hallelujah!" and other verbal encouragements. These comments are often very loud. We need to keep in mind that there was no amplification or microphones at the time and preachers had to call out the sermons to be heard. Charles Spurgeon once made the comment that, "if a man didn't have a huge barrel-shaped chest, God had not called him to preach." The congregants were merely responding at the same level as the preacher. This was not an occurrence in liturgical churches such as the Presbyterian churches, Reformed churches, or Northern Baptist churches, especially in churches with reflective acoustical buildings. After the Azusa St. Pentecostal out-pouring, verbal responses became more normal in the Pentecostal churches including the northern areas, but congregants are still very quiet north of the Bible belt.

We already referenced the Methodist paradigm against slavery initiated by John Wesley. We also spoke about the Great Awakening's effect on alerting churches about the tyranny of slavery that probably helped generate the Civil War. However, black and white churches in the North, though free, were also racially segregated. Black and white Christians have been kept separated since the Civil War by the Jim Crow laws, the lining out of hymns, the limited education of African-American pastors, and verbal responses in African-American churches, even in areas where Jim Crow laws were not in effect. These verbal, congregational, and worship traditions continue to divide black and white congregants even today in the modern church. Religious traditions prevent us from uniting as brothers and sisters in Christ. Maria Woodworth Etter's revivals also contain the history of black congregants attending. It was a blessing to see those historic assertions even in the southern states.

How Do We Unify?

There is only one thing that can bridge this racial and denominational divide. We must be willing to set aside our racial, denominational, and regional traditions of religion to come together as one body, the body of Christ. Do not mistake this for compromising anything that is the foundational truth of the gospel. Heresy remains heresy and compromise of gospel truth is heresy. But does any denominational sect represent God's entire truth? Absolutely not! We are not omniscient, omnipresent, or eternal. We are finite human beings who are able to only comprehend small portions of the Infinite.

When we condemn or exalt denominations, traditions, or liturgies, we have actually created an idol to worship. Loving other denominational believers in Christ and agreeing to the basic tenets of the gospel is essential to being unified as believers. Am I entitled to have opinions or beliefs that differ from yours? Absolutely, as long as they are based on scripture! But when I begin to condemn other people for scripture-based beliefs, I am judging them. Scripture makes it clear that there is only one person to whom we shall give account, and that is the God of Heaven! When we begin to condemn other people and denominations and say they are going to hell because they do not agree with our beliefs, we are attempting to take the place of Father God. We do not have the right to do that. We need to repent and take our proper place as the loving body of Christ. This repentance needs to start with pastoral leadership.

[1] Meltzer, Milton, <u>Hunted Like a Wolf, The Story of the Seminole War</u>, 1972, Farrar, Straus and Giroux, 19 Union Square, New York, NY 10003

CHAPTER 8

WHY THE CHURCH IS FAILING IN AMERICA

Looking at the back of someone's head in a worship service does not foster relational connections. Charisma magazine stated that 3700 churches closed their doors in America in 2015. According to Patheos.com, America has less than half of the churches it had 100 years ago. I do not think this has anything to do with the rise of mega churches. The organization National Black Robe Regiment (NBRR), cited a 2014 study that asserted 1.2 million people would leave the church in 2015. That is approximately 3,500 people per day. NBRR's estimation for 2015 church closings was 10,000. So what is driving this mass exodus from churches? I think there are several significant reasons that churches are dwindling and dying which we will attempt to address in this chapter. One reason many parishioners cited for leaving the church was not feeling they had any personal connections which we will address in the church's failure to make disciples.

The Church's Failure to Make Disciples

When we fail to obey Jesus' command to "go and make disciples," then we begin to look back on former moves of God to justify our church's existence. We begin to enshrine these revivals or moves of God. This is idolatry. A good historical example of this is the bronze serpent that Moses was commanded to form. The Israelites complained against God and Moses, and God sent venomous serpents among the people. Moses prayed to God for a solution for the people who were dying. God commanded him to make a bronze snake and put it on a pole. Anyone who was bitten and looked at the snake lived. Many years later King Hezekiah had to destroy the bronze snake because the Israelites were burning incense to it. This is exactly what we do when we claim past moves of God to vindicate our denominational churches rather than obeying God and moving forward and evangelizing and making disciples. The early church thrived because it was moving forward in obedience to God, but it took the persecution of Saul to actually get them to leave Jerusalem in obedience to Jesus' command, and go to Judea, Samaria, and the uttermost parts of the earth. In my opinion, God will allow the American church to undergo persecution if that's what it takes for us to obey him. It is our choice. What will we choose?

Before Jesus ascended into heaven, He gave his disciples this command, "Go into all the world and buy well-placed real estate, build spacious buildings with stained-glass windows, pipe organs, and spacious parking lots." Oops, sorry! I got that quote wrong. Let me try again. "Go into all the world and develop clever church programs that occupy people's time and keep them in the church building three or four days a week." Oh, I got it wrong again! What I meant to quote was, "Go into all the world and hire highly trained intellectual pastors who can fill people's minds with numerous facts about scripture." I hope that if you were in the same room with me and these words came out of my mouth, you would have the feeling that I should be slapped in the face! Matthew 28:18-20 is very simple and very clear, *"Then Jesus came to them and said, 'All authority in heaven and on earth has been given to me. Therefore go and make disciples of all nations, baptizing them in the name of the Father and of the Son and of the Holy Spirit, and teaching them to obey everything I have commanded you. And surely I am with you always, to the very end of the age.'"* The mission of the church is threefold; make disciples, baptize them, and personally demonstrate to them how to obey or follow Jesus. "Teaching them to obey," means show them how to do His works! If we want Jesus' presence with us, then this needs to be our first priority-MAKE DISCIPLES!

Conversion

So what is a disciple? Let's take a look at Jesus' example as He made disciples out of the ordinary people who followed Him.

First a disciple is someone who has received the gift of salvation by faith by believing that Jesus paid the price

91

as the Lamb of God for his or her sins. This forgiveness leads them into a relationship with Father God. So the first task of believers is to explain that God reconciled mankind to Himself through His Son Jesus Christ. It was not the intention of God that this should happen within the four walls of the church or at a once a year, three-day revival meeting. Every believer is called to be a witness for Jesus Christ in the workplace, in the marketplace, and in our homes. When believers fail to represent Jesus outside of the church, the church will die as it is doing in our nation.

When it comes to a Biblical example of conversion, we can look at the apostle Andrew's life. He was a follower of John the Baptist, but when John the Baptist said," *Look, the lamb of God who takes away the sin of the world,*" in reference to Jesus, Andrew immediately followed Jesus. He also went and found his brother Simon (Peter) and proclaimed that the Messiah had been found. Both of these men had already been baptized by John the Baptist. Eventually both of them became apostles, but not before they were disciples!

Baptism

We will not discuss the mode of baptism. Just do it! Jesus himself demonstrated the importance of baptism by submitting himself for baptism to John the Baptist prior to launching His ministry. After His own baptism, John chapter 3:22 says, *"After this, Jesus and his disciples went out into the Judean countryside, where he spent some time with them, and baptized."* This makes it very clear to us that Jesus himself baptized. After someone is converted to Christ, they are to be baptized. Then comes the hard part. They are to be personally discipled. I personally believe that the scripture makes it very plain that baptism follows conversion. If you believe in infant baptism I won't argue with you, but baptism is not a replacement for circumcision for a child. I still believe that if we baptize infants that when they come to personal faith they need to be re-baptized. We find no examples in Scripture of baptizing infants in spite of our church traditions. Please forgive me if I just offended you.

Discipleship

In Mark chapter 3:13-15, we find the specific calling of the 12 apostles. *"Jesus went up on a mountainside and called to him those He wanted, and they came to him. He appointed twelve that they might be with him and that He might send them out to preach and to have authority to drive out demons."* The part of this scripture that I find be significant to discipleship is the phrase, *"that they might be with him."* Discipleship is based on personal relationship. It is someone who has a vital relationship with Father God in prayer, personally coaching someone else to do the same thing, and to walk in the authority that God still bestows generously on all who are now indwelt by the Holy Spirit.

There were times when Jesus left his disciples and went up on a mountain to pray all night. He was setting an example for us to cultivate a life of prayer as His disciples. Jesus did attend synagogue services and heal and deliver people. He went to the temple in Jerusalem for the Jewish feasts, but when we read the New Testament, most of his encounters with people were outside in the public square. Many of these encounters also involved miracles. Five different verses in the King James Bible state that Jesus *"healed them all."* This had nothing to do with these people believing that Jesus was the Christ.

Jesus said in John 14:12-14, *"Very truly I tell you, whoever believes in me will do the works I have been doing, and they will do even greater things than these, because I am going to the Father. And I will do whatever you ask in my name, so that the Father may be glorified in the Son. You may ask me for anything in my name, and I will do it."* We have not discipled believers to walk in the power of God and do the works that Jesus did. We have failed! Many people who have left the church said they did so because they did not feel connected. This is a lack of discipleship and relational connections. I will say it again, looking at the back of someone's head in a worship service does not foster relational connections.

So how does discipleship multiply believers? Acts chapter 2:46-47 gives us an example of the formal and informal gatherings among the early believers: *"Every day they continued to meet together in the temple courts. They broke bread in their homes and ate together with glad and sincere hearts, praising God and enjoying the favor of all the people. And the Lord added to their number daily those who were being saved."* The temple courts provided an outdoor location where people could speak publicly to a crowd about a religious topic, but it is also obvious that there was an intimate fellowship as the early believers ate together in their homes. Many Bible scholars assert that this eating together was celebrating Holy Communion. Please notice that this fellowship of intimacy led many more people to faith in Christ, *"...And the Lord added to their number daily those who were being saved."* Keep in mind that there were no church buildings at this time. Church buildings appeared in 312 AD when Constantine converted to Christianity and made pagan temples into churches. Early believers gathered in synagogues or homes until unbelieving Jews kicked them out of the synagogues.

In many churches where I have spoken, I have asked the question, "How many people in this audience have ever been personally discipled?" Usually less than 2% of the congregation responds positively. We are not obeying Jesus command to go and make disciples. We are much more interested in getting church members who are willing to put money in an offering plate. This is rampant disobedience on the part of the body of Christ. If we expect to see revival in our nation, we must immediately address this lack of discipleship in our churches. We must come into obedience to our Lord's command!

CHAPTER 9

THE CHURCH AS A BUSINESS

One of the healthiest churches in the world is the underground Church in Communist China. It is estimated that Christian expansion in China is now at 10,000 new converts every day (World Evangelization Research Center). In my opinion, the vibrant growth and health of the Chinese Church has to do with their meeting in homes. These face-to-face encounters create relational connections and aid in discipling others. The Western Church is losing over 3,500 people per day, that is quite a contrast to our brothers and sisters in China.

Here are a few random facts from the Internet (some are outdated) on how Christians and North American churches spend their money:

- Christians' annual [worldwide] income is $12.3 trillion. $213 billion is given to Christian causes. $11.4 billion is given to foreign missions, 87% of which goes to work being done among the already Christian, 12% goes to work among the evangelized non-Christians, 1% among the un-evangelized. (The Traveling Team/TTT)

- Of foreign mission funding: 87% goes for work among those already Christian. 12% for work among already evangelized, but Non-Christian. 1% for work among the un-evangelized and unreached people. (Baxter 2007, 12)
- Christians make up 33% of the world's population, but receive 53% of the world's annual income and spend 98% of it on themselves. (Barrett and Johnson 2001, 656)
- Only .1% of all Christian giving is directed toward mission efforts in the 38 most un-evangelized countries in the world. (Barrett and Johnson 2001, 656)
- American Christians spend 95% of offerings on home-based ministry, 4.5% on cross-cultural efforts in already reached people groups, and .5% to reach the unreached. (TTT)
- Christians spend more on the annual audits of their churches and agencies ($810 million) than on all their workers in the non-Christian world. (World Evangelization Research Center/WERC)
- It costs Christians 700 times more money to baptize converts in rich Christian countries, such as Switzerland, [and America] than in poor un-evangelized countries, such as Nepal. (WERC)

When we examine the topic of money in the Western and European church, what we find is most of what we take in is spent on ourselves. Property maintenance and salaries is a huge chunk of this investment. Part of me wonders if Christianity became illegal in North America, and we were forced to meet secretly in homes, if our churches and relationships would not thrive as they are doing in the Chinese Church.

A pastor named Preston Sprinkle posted an online blog that I think it is very pertinent to this topic. He stated, *"The total income of American churchgoers is 5.2 trillion... It would take just a little over 1% of the income of American Christians to lift the poorest 1 billion people in the world out of extreme poverty...Have we made Christianity in America too expensive? Are we spending God's money on the things He would spend it on? Are all the resources (time, energy, personnel, and money) that go into pulling off church services every Sunday producing radical, Christ-like disciples? It just seems like we've created an expensive machine called "church" that's so dependent upon money (and lots of it) that it's hard to sustain or reproduce. And the return—making disciples who make disciples—has been far less than what we should expect."* His comments should cause us all to blush in shame. He is right! We have constructed a business enterprise that we now call "church." We are selfish, and self-centered! We are not producing disciples who are on fire for God.

Do we find any mention of real estate payments, pastoral salaries, secretarial salaries, worship leader salaries, or any other church positions mentioned in the New Testament? No, we don't. It is not wrong to support someone who has dedicated their life to ministry, and the apostle Paul makes that very clear in several of his epistles. But one of the main thrusts in the American church is paying for real estate and raising enough money to cover salaries for church staff and building upkeep. Is this really fulfilling the command to *"Go into all the world and make disciples?"* It is obvious from some of the statistics already quoted how little we spend on reaching unreached people groups. This is outright disobedience to Jesus' command to *"go into all the world."* There are countries where Westerners are not allowed to go, but that doesn't mean that we cannot find people in those countries whose ministries we could fund. The most disturbing quote in the financial statements above is the quote that there are 38 unreached countries, and we only spend .1% of our giving in our attempt to reach these countries with the gospel. Please notice that this financial quote is less than 1%; there is a decimal point in front of the number "one." That means we spend 99.9% of our money on ourselves! That is abysmal!

The Broken Methods of Appointing Pastors, Elders or Deacons

Pastors

We are making serious mistakes in the ways we appoint pastors. I Timothy chapter 3, And Titus chapter 1 are the two main passages that talk about how pastors or overseers should be chosen. It is interesting that we don't find any information about requiring a well-written resume in these passages. Neither do we find requirements for a Masters degree nor a Doctoral degree in divinity, nor do we find requirements for the letters of recommendation that we often expect, or referrals from previous positions. We do see New Testament examples of the apostle Paul recommending trusted disciples of his to churches, but these were traveling ministers. Pastors were already in place in most of these churches. What we do discover in these passages is that these people were chosen from the immediate surrounding body of Christ. Their lifestyle and their families were already known among those who were going to appoint them to positions of spiritual responsibility over the body of Christ. In many of our modern churches in America, pastors are distant, separate, and alienated from their congregations. Their families and their personal lives are not apparent to those around them. Many pastors and their families are required to put on a religious front. They are not allowed to be human. This is wrong!

I do not have a problem with educated pastors or training people for ministry. Most Americans do not speak Hebrew or Greek. We are not educated in the Old Testament as the early church, which was birthed out of synagogues and entrenched in Jewish teachings and spoke Greek (the language of the New Testament writings). We should also remember that Jesus had a very different method of choosing His own disciples. Many rabbis of the time chose the most talented students from the Jewish school system. The apostle Paul, the most prolific writer of the New Testament, was one of those students. But when we come to the other disciples of Jesus, we see four fishermen, a tax collector, a zealot, and other common men who would not have been chosen by other rabbis. Jesus' method for raising up leadership was discipling others to do what He did, and walking with them in relationship. After spending time in training His disciples, Jesus sent out 70 disciples and also the 12 apostles to the surrounding villages, commanding them to "heal the sick, cleanse lepers, and cast out demons." When they returned from this assignment, they reported that they had done all of those things. This was before Pentecost, before the Holy Spirit indwelt believers! Perhaps qualifying questions for pastors, elders, or deacons should follow Jesus' example: "When was the last time you saw someone healed, cleansed from an incurable disease, delivered from a demonic spirit, or raised from the dead?" I think that would eliminate a lot of candidates right up front before we read their resumes or heard them preach.

I have the privilege of being a member of a megachurch that chooses its pastoral staff, elders, and administrators from among the membership. We do have an advantage in these choices. Our main campus is less than a mile away from a Christian college and seminary. Many students attend our services while working on their degrees, but several of our pastors and staff members were actually reared in our church. We knew these people before we hired them, and we were familiar with their lifestyles and families. Some of our pastors do not have formal educations in all ministry topics, but they were ministering in the gospel to people before they were hired. Our senior pastor often hosts a life group meeting in his own home. He does not hide from regular people. There is a transparency on our pastoral staff to also share with our elders or life group members their family struggles, personal struggles, and other situations that need counsel and prayer. Our staff does not try to be superhuman or put on religious masks, or hide from the congregation. These are real families with real problems that find real solutions. And they share their journeys with the congregation while encouraging them to find solutions in Christ as they share their journey with others!

Elders or Deacons

Some denominational churches have both elders and deacons. Others have one or the other. I really don't care what your denomination does. What I care about is how you appoint those in spiritual leadership. Nor are we going to discuss the gender of elders or deacons. You may follow your denominational rules on that, or you can read the Scriptures, which make it plain that Paul welcomed women in the ministry. I have lived in five American states, two foreign countries, and experienced almost every denominational congregation possible as a worship leader for United States Army chaplains. I have over 18 years service to chapels and churches. I've also attended and visited numerous denominational churches as a congregant. In the appointing of elders or deacons, many churches that I have experienced look for men or women who are successful in business. That's because we have made a business paradigm of the Western church. We are appointing CEOs and their board members, not elders or deacons. We want people who can manage finances and keep our churches from going bankrupt. This has nothing to do with the scriptural qualifications for elders or deacons. I've seen churches where elders or deacons controlled the entire church and manipulated pastors and congregations by controlling the money. That is wrong!

In addition to the qualifications for these positions found in I Timothy chapter 3 and Titus chapter 1, we see the first deacons were originally appointed to care for the poor people and widows from the donations that were being made by the early church as believers sold property and possessions. The deacons were appointed to relieve the Apostles of these financial burdens so they might give their attention to the ministry of the Word and prayer. These men were trusted individuals who were full of faith and good works. In addition to Paul's qualifications for these offices, Acts 6:3 states the first qualifications: *"Brothers and sisters, choose seven men from among you who are known to be full of the spirit and wisdom..."* Please notice the men were chosen by the brothers and sisters; they were not appointed by the apostles. The first martyr of the church, Stephen, was an appointed deacon. In Acts chapter 8 we see the story of Philip who was also an appointed deacon. One of the characteristics we see in Phillip's life was his performance of signs, miracles, and wonders. This was in addition to his financial fidelity. Do we see this in our elders and deacons that we appoint today? If this qualified those first appointed, should it not qualify those we appoint? Our deacons and elders should be full of the Holy Spirit and wisdom, in addition for us to trust them with our business transactions. It is not success in business or money that first qualifies them for these positions, but it is their proven spiritual life in addi-tion to their trustworthiness. Perhaps our first questions qualifying candidates for elders or deacons like pastoral candidates also should be, "When was the last time you saw someone saved, healed, or delivered?" If they cannot respond to that question positively, they're not qualified for the office according to Scripture.

Tithes, Offerings and Missionaries

We need to take a new look at our budgets. Tithing originated before the Mosaic Law was given and continues as an ongoing biblical principle. One of our first examples of tithing was when Abraham gave a tenth of the spoils to Melchizedek. Jesus also put a stamp of approval on tithing when He was rebuking the Pharisees. In Matthew 23:23 He stated, *"Woe to you, teachers of the law and Pharisees, you hypocrites! You give a tenth of your spices—mint, dill and cumin. But you have neglected the more important matters of the law—justice, mercy and faithfulness. You should have practiced the latter, without neglecting the former."* This is obviously an affirmation of tithing, and a rebuke on religious traditions.

Part of the problem with modern-day teaching on tithing is the emphasis that many churches seem to assert that the entire tithe should support the church budget. We do not see this in early New Testament collections. Believers were collecting money to support widows, people who were starving in famines, and supporting ministries that were spreading the gospel. In many churches that I have attended, all missionary giving is supposed to be over and above the tithe. It is often called "faith giving," or some other form of a name that indicates it is not a part of my tithe. Can anyone quote me any New Testament scripture that has anything to do with this concept of selfishness? Once again we're back to the problem that the American church spends its money on itself rather than making disciples. We need to take a new look at our budgets. Not only should we fund evangelism around our churches and neighborhoods, feed the poor, and care for widows, but also we should be reaching the unreached people groups. The Baxter quote on our church giving stated that we only spent .1% of our budgets on reaching those who have never heard the gospel. Is anyone content with that figure? Is that obedience to our Lord's command to *"go into all the world and make disciples?"* I hope this generates some serious discussions among church boards and congregations and changes the selfish way we spend our money.

CHAPTER 10

HOW DO WE INITIATE REVIVAL?

Repentance and Confession

I have read many histories of revivals throughout the world. Revival starts with God's people, the church, turning from their sins in repentance and confession. Chapters 3, 4, and 5 list many of the things that need to be addressed in repentance in the body of Christ. There are also more sins that need to be addressed other than what I covered. The verse on the cover of this book is very important to apply to our lives to see revival in America. *II Chronicles 7:14, "If My people, who are called by My name, will humble themselves and pray, and seek My face and turn from their wicked ways, then I will hear from heaven, and will forgive their sin and will heal their land."* Some of our previous chapters highlighted the sin that is bringing judgment on America. To my knowledge there has never been a great revival that was not characterized by passionate prayer and the oral confession of sin to fellow believers. To me, "humbling ourselves" means throwing down our religious masks while being real and transparent with one another as we confess our sins to one another. Too many people in the church are terrified of rejection if they become known in their struggles. That's because we have failed to make disciples and cultivate transparent relationships.

Dietrich Bonhoeffer was martyred by the Nazis for challenging their imprisonment of Jews and being part of a plot to assassinate Hitler. He wrote a book entitled Life Together while he was in prison. Bonhoeffer has a fascinating quote about oral confession of sin which has to do with "humbling ourselves" from his book. Bonhoeffer asserts, *"In confession a man breaks through to certainty. Why is it that it is often easier for us to confess our sins to God than to a brother? Why should we not find it easier to go to a brother than to the holy God? But if we do, we must ask ourselves whether we have not often been deceiving ourselves with our confession of sin to God, whether we have not rather been confessing our sin to ourselves and also granting ourselves absolution."*

Having been reared in a Baptist church, I often heard pastors railing against Catholic confession booths and condemning the oral confession of sin. This was a wrong teaching. James 5:14-20 makes it very plain that confessing our sins to trustworthy, spiritual people, not a priest in a covered booth, is a normal part of the Christian life. *"Is anyone among you sick? Let them call the elders of the church to pray over them and anoint them with oil in the name of the Lord. And the prayer offered in faith will make the sick person well; the Lord will raise them up. If they have sinned, they will be forgiven. Therefore confess your sins to each other and pray for each other that you may be healed. The prayer of a righteous person is powerful and effective. Elijah was a human being, even as we are. He prayed earnestly that it would not rain, and it did not rain on the land for three and a half years. Again he prayed and the heavens gave rain, and the earth produced its crops. My brothers and sisters, if one of you should wander from the truth and someone should bring that person back, remembers this: whoever turns a sinner from the error of their way will save them from death and cover a multitude of sins."* Some may assert that this confession has to do with physical healing and it does, but the remainder of the passage also makes it clear that it has to do with repentance and turning from sin.

So you do you need more scriptural proof? One of the most common verses quoted about confession of sin is I John 1:9, *"If we confess our sins, He is faithful and just and will forgive us our sins and purify us from all unrighteousness."* When we read the entire chapter we discover that's the theme is fellowship with God and with one another. Let me ask you a question about   I John 1:9. Are the pronouns singular or plural? They are plural! I think this suggests confession to one another, not solo confession to God at the altar. I found in private confession, that I was always confessing the same sin. I kept repeating my sin, because I had not made myself accountable to anyone for spiritual support. In a discipleship relationship when I confess my faults I have also, hopefully, found a support partner to encourage me and help me learn to overcome my sin by putting on Christ.

Are you still not convinced? Acts chapter 19 gives us the story of Paul's visit to Ephesus. Verses 17 through 20 give us specific examples of oral confession of sin: *"When this became known to the Jews and Greeks living in Ephesus, they were all seized with fear, and the name of the Lord Jesus was held in high honor. Many of those who believed now came and openly confessed what they had done. A number who had practiced sorcery brought their scrolls together and burned them publicly. When they calculated the value of the scrolls, the total came to fifty thousand drachmas. In this way the word of the Lord spread widely and grew in power."* I am convinced that if we want to see the Word of the Lord spread and grow in power as it did in this passage, we need to practice the oral confession of sin to one another.

This is a slap in the face to many of my dear Protestant brothers and sisters, but it is a characteristic of revival. As you know from our previous discussion, John Wesley was kicked out of the Anglican Church after his conversion when he began to preach with passion and fire. Those that were converted to Christ had to meet in their own homes because they were not welcome in the Anglican Church buildings. Here is Wesley's command to his home groups. First of all he said that the men and women were to meet separately. He then gave his home groups these four questions or directives to share with one another as they met:

1. *"'What known sins have you committed since our last meeting?'*
2. *'What temptations have you met with?'*
3. *'How were you delivered?'*
4. *'What have you thought, said or done of which you doubt whether it be sin or not?'"*

Wesley did not just deal with known sin; he also dealt with temptations and questionable areas. Dealing with thoughts and imaginations can also be very important. As you already know this revival swept through Great Britain and also influenced the American colonies through men like Francis Asbury, George Whitfield and Jonathan Edwards.

If you read the history of Charles Finney's revivals, you will discover that pastors and church leaders we're some of the first to stand and orally confess their sins to their congregations. There were also side rooms called "mourners rooms." This was a room where people could go to receive ministry and also orally confess their sins as they repented or came to faith in Christ while the service was ongoing.

The Welsh revival which was birthed by Evan Roberts, was launched by Roberts reading these four simple principles to a group of young people:

(1) Confess all known sin to God, receiving forgiveness through Jesus Christ.
(2) Remove anything from your life that you are in doubt or feel unsure about.
(3) Be totally yielded and obedient to the Holy Spirit.
(4) Publicly confess the Lord Jesus Christ.

Please notice that the first principle was the confession of sin, and this was done in a public manner. If you are still not convinced that the oral confession of sin is necessary to revival, then begin reading revival histories. You will become convinced that it is a necessity.

The problem for most of us with Protestant backgrounds is that we don't know how to do this. Let me give you a very simple paradigm. Follow Wesley's rule and divide men and women into two separate groups. Explain to your small group of men or women to picture Jesus in their imagination individually taking their sin. Some may want to picture Him on the cross. Some may want to see Him seated at the right hand of the Father in heaven. Some may have other imaginations. It doesn't matter. Then just ask them to lay their sins on Jesus, the Lamb of God. Ask them to use Biblical words to describe their sin as best they can. For example Scripture calls marital unfaithfulness adultery, not an affair. Explain before you begin that they are not to pray for themselves or pronounce forgiveness over themselves. That is the job of the brothers or sisters around them. When they are finished confessing, ask them if they will receive Father God's forgiveness. When they affirm that they will receive God's promise of forgiveness, assert as their brother or sister in Christ that you do not hold these things that they have confessed against them. Then pronounce a Scripture verse over them that affirms God's forgiveness. For example, Psalm 103:12 says, *"...as far as the east is from the west, so far has He removed our transgressions from us."* You don't have to know the book, chapter, and verse, but make sure you pronounce God's forgiveness over the brother or sister scripturally. The freedom that oral confession brings is amazing! It breaks people free from shame, destroys religious posturing, and develops intimate relationships. It also develops trusted relationships where people are free to share their life struggles and find out how to be victorious in Christ.

Prayer

I have the privilege of membership at a church that highly exalts prayer. We are a multi-campus church, and every location has an early morning prayer meeting starting at 6:30 AM at least one day a week. Additionally there are soaking prayer evening sessions at each campus. Our congregation is also organized into a 24/7 prayer watch, which happens individually in our homes. We also host extended worship and intercession services in the church building patterned after the IHOP model. The entire month of August is spent with special prayer meetings and fasting in preparation for the launch of our life group ministry and the start of schooling for our children. So are we seeing revival? Not yet. But we are sowing the seeds and as a farm-boy, I know they will grow.

As I read revival history, I have also realized that revivals are birthed through fervent prayer for an outpouring of God. One of the most amazing American revival histories was "The Laymen's Prayer Revival" 1857-1858. America was in an abysmal place morally, especially with alcohol, and one man decided to start a prayer meeting. There is a wonderful, concise history of the move online at: http://www.praywithchrist.org/prayer/layman.php This revival had no famous speakers or evangelists. This movement began at a time when America was entrenched in alcoholism. It was completely led by laymen as God's Spirit began to fall on the masses as people prayed. This prayer revival swept from New York throughout the mid-western territories, which were not yet states, all the way to California. Here's a quote from the online article about the beginning of the

113

revival: *"America's moral recovery began when Jeremiah Lanphier, a concerned layman, started a noon prayer meeting for New York businessmen. Only six people came to the first prayer meeting on September 23, 1857 on the third floor of the 'Consistory' of the Old Dutch Reformed Church on Fulton Street. By spring daily prayer meetings sprang up in many locations and daily attendance grew to 10,000. America's greatest Spiritual awakening was under way. It was called the Layman's Prayer Revival because laymen led it."*

This move of the Spirit of God and the manifest presence of God was so powerful that ships coming into New York harbor had sailors fall to their knees and repent and receive Christ with no one speaking to them. This same phenomenon occurred during the Charles Finney revivals because he was so full of the presence of God from his prayer life. Finney walked into a factory being led by the owner going to his office to have a conversation. As Finney walked through the workspace, men fell to their knees and began to weep, repenting of their sin. Finney had not spoken a word. He was so saturated by prayer in the presence of God that these men were overwhelmed by that presence. The prayers and tears of these people created an atmosphere where God was moving in power. Is anyone else hungry and thirsty for that kind of presence?

Joseph Mattera wrote an online article for Charisma magazine outlining the dangers of a non-praying church. Please take note of his assertion that members are not discipled when a church does not pray. The article is entitled "10 Hazards of the Prayerless Church." The entire article is readable at: http://www.charismanews.com/opinion/the-pulse/59918-10-hazards-of-the-prayerless-church?

Here are the basic warnings from his article:
1. A prayerless church demonstrates that the leaders are prayerless.
2. They don't hear what the Spirit is saying.
3. There is a lack of true oneness.
4. There is a lack of divine intervention from intercession.
5. There is a lack of the presence and power of God that sustains ministry.
6. The knowledge of God is superficial.
7. The members are not made into disciples.
8. They don't uncover the enemy's schemes.
9. The leaders are building in vain.
10. There is a huge gap in the armor of God.

So how do we engender revival? We must form prayer meetings completely dedicated to humbling ourselves before God, confessing the sins of the church and our nation, and asking him to pour out a Spirit of conviction, first upon believers, and secondly on unbelievers as we go with the Gospel. When I was a child in the 1950s, there was a Wednesday night prayer meeting in almost every church in our area. They really were prayer meetings. People got together, shared prayer requests, and prayed. By the 1960s these prayer meetings dwindled and became Wednesday night Bible studies. Many churches lost the fervency for prayer in America, exchanging it for intellectual knowledge about scripture.

As we were recently organizing ourselves into small groups to pray for revival for America at a support group meeting a friend of mine stated, "Praying for national revival is fine, but revival needs to start in our own homes."

He was right. So first of all let's organize our own personal time to call out to God for repentance and revival for our nation. Secondly, are there prodigal sons and daughters in our own homes who need our prayers to turn back to God? Thirdly, organize our families to pray and intercede for our nation during our family devotional time as we read the word of God and pray together. If you have a family and you are not doing these things, may I suggest that you organize your family around the Word and prayer?

Next start with inviting your pastor and church leaders to form prayer gatherings. Please attempt to inform them about the importance of confession and revival. Perhaps you could loan them this book. Try to find other believers in your congregation who also have a passion to see a move of God. Organize a prayer meeting either in your home, or in your church. Center your prayers on II Chronicles 7:14. Begin practicing the oral confession of sin together. As you confess our national sins, confess them as your own. Intercession means "to stand in someone else's shoes," so let us "own" our national sins as if we had committed them.

Many areas now also have 24/7 (twenty-four hours a day, seven days a week) prayer movements patterned after Count Von Zinzendorf's revival in Herrnhut, Germany. Mike Bickle at the International House of Prayer (IHOP) in Kansas City, Missouri brought this movement back to life in America. Their meeting is streamed live on the Internet. The style of prayer and worship may differ from location to location, but the thrust is similar. There is usually a background of worship music with a room full of people seeking God in prayer during the worship. There are times of oral reading of scripture, open microphones for intercessions, or other variants to the worship and intercession base. Many of these houses of prayer actually have sign-up sheets for different hours of the day. Be a volunteer or start your own extended prayer meeting! It doesn't have to go 24/7 to be effective.

How Do We Pray?

As I already mentioned, we need to confess our country's sins as if they were our own. The book of Daniel chapter 9:4b-19 has a wonderful example of a prayer of repentance. Daniel had been reading the prophet Jeremiah and understood that the diaspora [scattering of Israel] would last for 70 years. He began fasting and praying while clothing himself in sackcloth as he repented for Israel. I personally took Daniel's prayer and modified it for America. I have prayed Daniel's prayer aloud in revival prayer meetings and daily in my prayer time. I think Daniel's model gives us a good basis on how to pray for our country. I would suggest inserting particular confessions of sin that cover our nation's transgressions. Here is the paraphrase I designed from Daniel's prayer.

"LORD, the great and awesome God, who keeps his covenant of love with those who love him and keep his commandments, we Americans have sinned and done wrong. We have been wicked and have rebelled; we have turned away from your commands and laws. We have not listened to your servants, who spoke in your name to our leaders, our ancestors, and to all the people of the land. LORD, you are righteous, but this day we are covered with shame—the people of America and of our states because of our unfaithfulness to you. We and our leaders and our ancestors are covered with shame, LORD, because we have

sinned against you. The LORD our God is merciful and for-giving, even though we have rebelled against him; we have not obeyed the LORD our God or kept the laws he gave us through his servants. All America has transgressed your law and turned away, refusing to obey you. Therefore the curses and sworn judgments written in the Law of Moses, the servant of God, have been poured out on us, because we have sinned against you. You have fulfilled the words spoken against us and against our leaders by bringing on us great disaster. Except for Israel, nothing has ever been done like what has been done to America. Just as it is written in the Law of Moses, all this disaster has come on us, yet we have not sought the favor of the LORD our God by turning from our sins and giving attention to your truth. The LORD did not hesitate to bring the disaster on us, for the LORD our God is righteous in everything he does; yet we have not obeyed him. Now, LORD our God, who brought your people out of many nations with a mighty hand and who made for yourself a name that endures to this day in America, we have sinned, we have done wrong. LORD, in keeping with all your righteous acts, turn away your anger and your wrath from America. Our sins and the iniquities of our ancestors have made America and your people an object of scorn to all those around us. Now, our God, hear the prayers and petitions of your servants. For your sake, Lord, look with favor on your desolate country. Give ear, our God, and hear; open your eyes and see the desola-tion of the country that bears your name. We do not make requests of you because we are righteous, but because of your great mercy. LORD, listen! LORD, forgive! LORD, hear and act! For your sake, our God, do not delay, because this country and your people bear your Name."

CHAPTER 11

WHAT WILL REVIVAL LOOK LIKE?

I thought the previous chapter was the end of my book. God had a different thought. When I asked Him if I was done, and should I submit the book to a publisher; the Lord told me to finish reading the book of Ezekiel. I resumed reading where I had finished the day before at chapter 40, and read through the end of the book. Chapter 40 begins the restoration of Jerusalem, the temple, and the return of the presence of God to the temple. God spoke to me about restoring His Church in America. I believe God wants to see it happen! I believe that God wants to restore the fervency and the gifting of the early church to America, but I believe He wants to do much more than that! If you do not believe in the gifts of the Spirit, you will find this chapter insulting. I was reared as a cessationist Baptist. I was taught that the apostles did signs and wonders, and that when they died, the gospel had been established and signs and wonders were no longer needed. If that's what you believe, God bless you. Then at least respond to the call of this book to make disciples and begin evangelizing! But if you believe the Bible is the word of God, do you believe what Jesus said in John 14:12-14? *"Very truly I tell you, whoever believes in me will do the works I have been doing, and they will do even greater things than these, because I am going to the Father. And I will do whatever you ask in my name, so that the Father may be glorified in the Son. You may ask me for anything in my name, and I will do it."* I don't think the word "whoever" refers only to the apostles. I think it refers to every believer in Jesus Christ.

I believe the passage in Joel 2:28-32 refers to the coming of Jesus, not just a restoration of Jerusalem, but I believe this outpouring of the Spirit precedes His coming: *"And afterward, I will pour out my Spirit on all people. Your sons and daughters will prophesy, your old men will dream dreams, your young men will see visions. Even on my servants, both men and women, I will pour out my Spirit in those days. I will show wonders in the heavens and on the earth, blood and fire and billows of smoke. The sun will be turned to darkness and the moon to blood before the coming of the great and dreadful day of the* LORD. *And everyone who calls on the name of the* LORD *will be saved; for on Mount Zion and in Jerusalem there will be deliverance, as the* LORD *has said, even among the survivors whom the* LORD *calls."* This passage specifically states, *"I will pour out my Spirit on all people."* If any of you have any involvement with missionary endeavors among Muslims, you are aware of visions of Jesus that unbelieving Muslims have experienced. This outpouring is happening now! These visions, like the apostle Paul's vision of Jesus, have led many Muslims to Christ. If you don't believe what I've written, simply do an Internet search for "visions of Jesus by Muslims." You will find innumerable stories and news reports by both missionaries, and Muslims now living in free countries who are able to share their testimonies without fear of assassination.

Can you imagine "greater works" than what Jesus performed? He promised that we would do them because He was going to the Father. The same spirit that raised Jesus from The dead is in us. Why then are we not seeing these greater works? I believe it is because of our unbelief, and our religious traditions, and our failure to disciple believers. Are apostles, evangelists, and those with the gift of miracles the only persons who are to experience people being healed, delivered from demonic spirits, cured of incurable diseases, or raised from the dead? Absolutely not! Jesus promised, *"...whoever believes in me will do the works that I have been doing."*

Jesus proclaimed his utter dependency on the Father in John 5:19 when He stated, *"Very truly I tell you, the Son can do nothing by himself; He can do only what he sees his Father doing, because whatever the father does the Son also does."* Relationship with our heavenly Father is not just reading scripture. Jesus said, *"my sheep hear my voice, and they follow me."* Are you personally hearing God's voice? I know that this statement is absolutely terrifying to those of you from cessationist backgrounds. I was taught that God only spoke to us as we read His word. That is not true. John chapter 6:5 tells us that Jesus asked Philip, "Where shall we buy bread for these people to eat?" But the narrative goes on to explain that Jesus already had in mind what He was going to do. He had already heard the father. He multiplied the barley loaves and fish and fed the multitude.

Modern Day Examples of the Miraculous

The country of Mozambique, Africa, was previously predominantly Muslim or pagan. Not anymore! Since 1994, Heidi and Roland Baker have created a network of more than 2,000 churches that walk in signs, wonders, and miracles. They have seen more than 200 people raised from the dead and that number is several years old! The Muslim Imams in Saudi Arabia discussed the loss of Mozambique to Christianity. They said, "What are we going to do? Christians are raising the dead! We have no defense against that." Entire villages are being evangelized as they experience miracles. One of the methods used by the ministry team in Mozambique is to take a flatbed truck and load it with the ministry partners. They then drive to an un-evangelized Muslim village. When they get to the village, they ask the villagers to bring out the deaf, the blind, and the lame. They lay hands on these people and proclaim healing. Immediately following this healing ministry, they quickly board the truck and drive off so they won't be stoned to death when the Moslem villagers find out they are Christians. After several weeks they return to the village. After the deaf have been hearing, the blind seeing, and the lame walking for several weeks, the villagers are ready to hear that it was Jesus who healed them. Entire Muslim villages overwhelmingly turn their lives over to Christ. So are miracles not needed anymore since the apostles are dead? Why don't you answer that obvious question yourself based on the conversion of an entire country! Obviously God still uses miracles to show His love and power.

Greater Works

Let your imagination run wild! What are some miracles you can think of that Jesus did not do? Can we imagine missing limbs growing out for those with birth defects, or soldiers who have lost body parts in combat? Can we imagine major psychiatric disorders being healed on the spot and not throwing drugs at people to subjugate the disorder? Can we imagine retarded children or children with Downs syndrome being healed on the spot as their defects are healed or their genes restored? Can we imagine homosexuals with AIDS being healed? I don't think it is God's will for anyone to come into our churches in pain, with an incurable disease, with a missing limb, or with a mental disorder to leave the same way! And that is just my imagination! What can you imagine? Not only should miracles be happening in our churches, but also they should be happening in the workplace, on the streets, on our shopping trips, and in our homes!

Some of you might be thinking whether or not I have seen this take place. The answer is yes! I saw a woman in her 30s, who had been blind in one eye since she was two years old after a surgeon accidentaly severed her optic nerve, have her eyesight totally restored in my business office. I've seen God empty wheelchairs. An unbelieving Muslim lady, whose knee had been injured in a car accident, was healed on my front lawn when I proclaimed healing over her knee in the name of "Isa," the Muslim name for Jesus. I have a list of miracles that I've seen God do as I ministered His love and power to others in the marketplace, in my home, and at church. But I want more! Do you? I want to be a walking demonstration of Father God's love and power! Are you thirsty to see the power of God released in your life, on the streets, in your place of business, and in your church? If one person begins to burn with the power of God in his or her life, others who rub up against him or her who are dry and parched will be ignited to burn with the same fire. Or they have the choice to turn away in disgust like the Pharisees and Sadducees and return to their religious traditions. Are you choosing to burn, or to worship the denominational idol we have created in the Western Church? The choice is ours. Please choose to burn with revival fire!

BIBLIOGRAPHY

All scripture quotations in this publication, unless otherwise noted, are from the HOLY BIBLE, NEW INTERNATIONAL VERSION ® NIV ® Copyright ©1973, 1978, 1984, 2011 by Biblica, Inc.®. Used by permission. All rights reserved worldwide.

Bonhoeffer, Dietrich, Life Together: The Classic Exploration of Christian Community, Copyright © 1954 by Harper & Row Publishers, Inc. All rights reserved. Printed in the United States of America. Harper Collins Publishers, 10 East 53rd Street, New York, NY 10022.

Easton, Matthew George, Easton's Bible Dictionary, [Illustrated Bible Dictionary], (1897), is in the public domain and may be freely used and distributed.

Jewish Encyclopedia (1901-1906) The Jewish Encyclopedia is in the public domain and may be freely used and distributed.

Meltzer, Milton, Hunted Like a Wolf, The Story of the Seminole War, 1972, Farrar, Straus and Giroux, 19 Union Square, New York, NY 10003

Merriam-Webster's Collegiate® Dictionary, 11th Edition ©2016 by Merriam-Webster, Inc. (www.Merriam-Webster.com)

Orr, James, editor, International Standard Bible Encyclopedia, 1939, William B. Erdmans publishing company, 2140 Oak Industrial Dr. NE, Grand Rapids, MI 49505

Strong, James, Strong's Concordance with Hebrew and Greek Lexicon, 1890, is in the public domain and may be freely used and distributed.

Thayer, Joseph Henry, Thayer's Greek Lexicon, 1889, is in the public domain and may be freely used and distributed.

Webster's New World Dictionary: Third College Edition, Webster's New World Dictionaries, copyright © 1988 a division of Simon and Schuster Inc., Gulf+Western Building, Gulf+Western Plaza, New York, NY 10023

CPSIA information can be obtained
at www.ICGtesting.com
Printed in the USA
FFOW05n0746170317